KUNAR PROVINCE, AFGHANISTAN...
"I FEEL LIKE YOU'RE DRIVIN' ME TO A COURT MARTIAL. WHAT, YOU'RE NOT ALLOWED TO TALK?"
"WE CAN TALK, MR STARK."
"SO IT'S PERSONAL?"
SIR, IS IT TRUE YOU WENT TWELVE FOR TWELVE WITH LAST YEAR'S MAXIM COVER MODELS?
YES AND NO. MARCH AND I HAD A SCHEDULING CONFLICT, BUT FORTUNATELY THE CHRISTMAS COVER WAS TWINS. ANYTHING ELSE?
IS IT COOL IF I TAKE A PICTURE WITH YOU?
YES, IT'S VERY COOL.
PLEASE, NO GANG SIGNS.
NO, THROW IT UP, I'M KIDDING.
YEAH, "PEACE." I LOVE PEACE. I'D BE OUT OF A JOB WITH PEACE.
D0124160
CONTACT LEFT! CONTACT LEFT!
BRRROOM
JIMMY! STAY WITH STARK!
SON OF A--!
ARRRRHHHHH!!

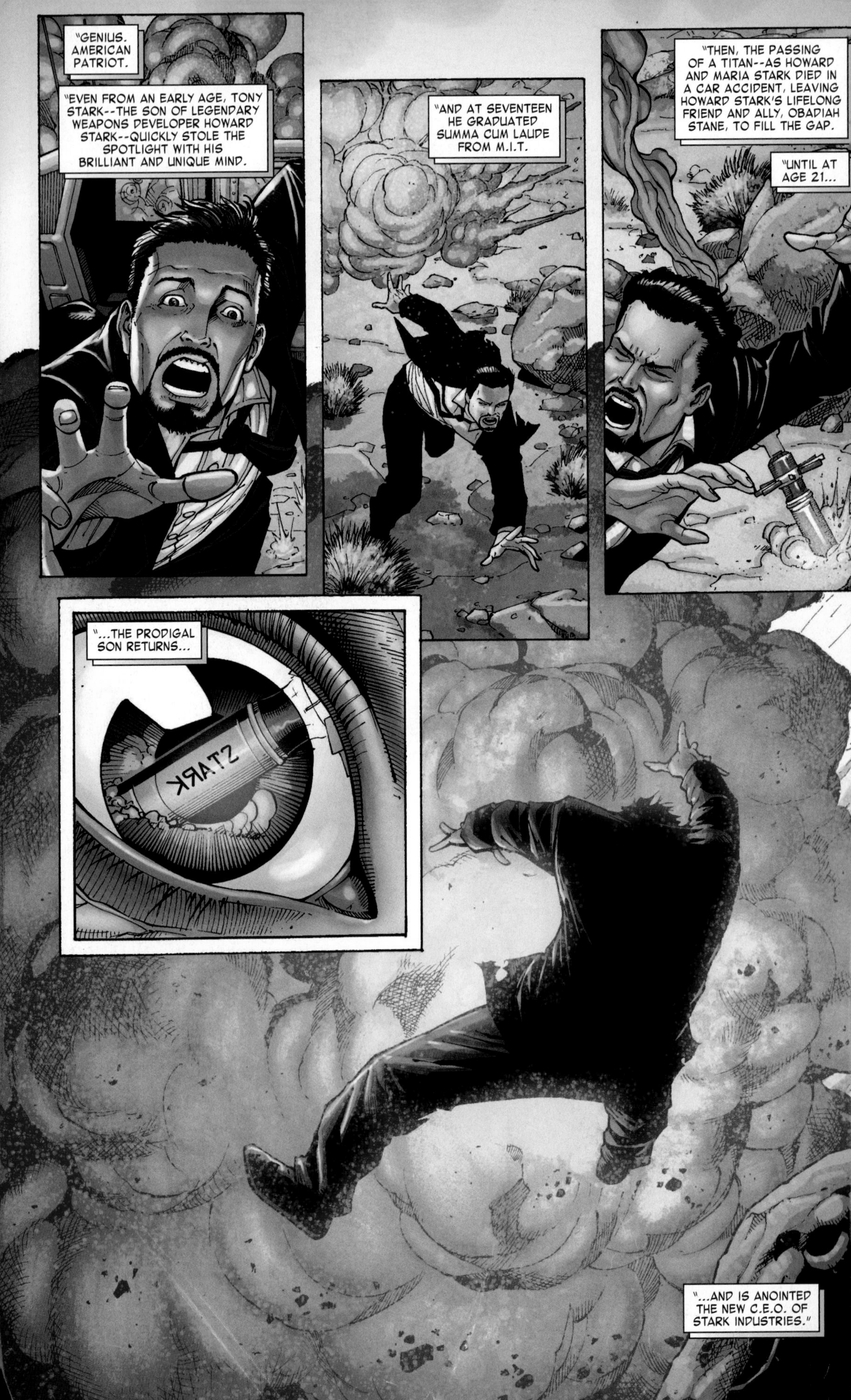
"GENIUS. AMERICAN PATRIOT.
"EVEN FROM AN EARLY AGE, TONY STARK--THE SON OF LEGENDARY WEAPONS DEVELOPER HOWARD STARK--QUICKLY STOLE THE SPOTLIGHT WITH HIS BRILLIANT AND UNIQUE MIND.
"AND AT SEVENTEEN HE GRADUATED SUMMA CUM LAUDE FROM M.I.T.
"THEN, THE PASSING OF A TITAN--AS HOWARD AND MARIA STARK DIED IN A CAR ACCIDENT, LEAVING HOWARD STARK'S LIFELONG FRIEND AND ALLY, OBADIAH STANE, TO FILL THE GAP.
"UNTIL AT AGE 21...
"...THE PRODIGAL SON RETURNS...
STARK
"...AND IS ANOINTED THE NEW C.E.O. OF STARK INDUSTRIES."

NOW...
THEN...
"AS LIAISON TO STARK INDUSTRIES, I'VE HAD THE UNIQUE PRIVILEGE OF SERVING WITH A REAL PATRIOT. HE IS MY FRIEND AND HE IS MY GREAT MENTOR.
"LADIES AND GENTLEMEN, IT IS MY HONOR TO PRESENT THIS YEAR'S APOGEE AWARD TO MISTER TONY STARK.
"...
"...TONY...?"
COME

YOU ARE UNBELIEVABLE.
THEY TOLD ME THAT IF I PRESENTED YOU WITH AN AWARD, YOU WOULD BE DEEPLY HONORED.
OF COURSE I'D BE DEEPLY HONORED, RHODEY. SO WHEN DO WE DO IT?

THERE IT IS. *THAT* WAS EASY.
THIS IS WHERE I EXIT. DON'T BE LATE TOMORROW.

"YEAH, YOU CAN COUNT ON IT, RHODEY."
MISTER STARK! CHRISTINE EVERHART, *VANITY FAIR!* CAN I ASK YOU A COUPLE OF QUESTIONS?
OKAY, GO.

YOU'VE BEEN CALLED THE DA VINCI OF OUR TIME. WHAT DO YOU SAY TO THAT?
ABSOLUTELY RIDICULOUS. I DON'T PAINT.
AND WHAT DO YOU SAY TO YOUR OTHER NICKNAME: "*THE MERCHANT OF DEATH*"?
THAT'S NOT BAD.
ALL I WANT IS A SERIOUS ANSWER.
TELL ME, DO YOU PLAN TO REPORT ON THE MILLIONS OF LIVES WE'VE SAVED BY ADVANCING MEDICAL TECHNOLOGY, OR KEPT FROM STARVATION WITH OUR INTELLI-CROPS? ALL THOSE BREAK-THROUGHS: MILITARY FUNDING, HONEY.
WOW. YOU EVER LOSE AN HOUR OF SLEEP IN YOUR WHOLE LIFE?

I'D BE PREPARED TO LOSE A FEW WITH YOU.

GOOD MORNING. IT'S SEVEN A.M. THE WEATHER IN MALIBU IS SEVENTY-TWO DEGREES WITH SCATTERED CLOUDS. THE SURF CONDITIONS ARE FAIR WITH WAIST-TO-SHOULDER-HIGH LINES.
HUH?
HIGH TIDE WILL BE AT TEN FIFTY-TWO A.M.
TONY?
THAT'S J.A.R.V.I.S. HE RUNS THE HOUSE.
I'VE GOT YOUR CLOTHES HERE. THEY'VE BEEN DRY-CLEANED AND PRESSED, AND THERE'S A CAR WAITING OUTSIDE THAT WILL TAKE YOU ANYWHERE YOU'D LIKE TO GO.
YOU MUST BE THE FAMOUS PEPPER POTTS.
INDEED I AM.
AFTER ALL THESE YEARS, TONY STILL HAS YOU PICKING UP THE DRY-CLEANING.
I DO ANYTHING AND EVERYTHING THAT MISTER STARK REQUIRES, INCLUDING, OCCASIONALLY...
...TAKING OUT THE TRASH.

HOW'D SHE TAKE IT?
LIKE A CHAMP. YOUR FLIGHT WAS SCHEDULED TO LEAVE AN HOUR AND A HALF AGO.
I THOUGHT, WITH IT BEING MY PLANE AND ALL, THAT IT WOULD JUST WAIT FOR ME TO GET THERE.
I NEED YOU TO SIGN THIS BEFORE YOU GET ON THE PLANE.

WHAT ARE YOU TRYIN' TO GET RID OF ME FOR? HAVE YOU GOT PLANS?
I'M ALLOWED TO HAVE PLANS ON MY BIRTHDAY.
IT'S YOUR BIRTHDAY?
YES.

I KNEW THAT. GET YOURSELF SOMETHING NICE FROM ME.
YEAH?
I ALREADY DID. IT WAS VERY NICE.
VERY TASTEFUL.

THANK YOU, MISTER STARK.
YOU'RE WELCOME, MISS POTTS.

"THEY SAY THE BEST WEAPON IS ONE YOU NEVER HAVE TO FIRE. I RESPECTFULLY DISAGREE. I PREFER THE WEAPON YOU ONLY HAVE TO FIRE *ONCE*. THAT'S HOW DAD DID IT. THAT'S HOW AMERICA DOES IT..."

AFGHANISTAN...

AND IT'S WORKED OUT PRETTY WELL SO FAR.

"WITH THAT IN MIND, I HUMBLY PRESENT THE CROWN JEWEL OF STARK INDUSTRIES' FREEDOM LINE. IT'S THE FIRST MISSILE SYSTEM TO INCORPORATE OUR PROPRIETARY REPULSOR TECHNOLOGY.

"FOR YOUR CONSIDERATION--"

THE JERICHO.

KATHOOOOOM

NOW...

WHAT'D I *DO?* WHAT I DID IS SAVE YOUR LIFE. I REMOVED ALL THE SHRAPNEL THAT I COULD, BUT THERE'S A LOT LEFT...

...AND IT'S HEADED INTO YOUR ATRIAL SEPTUM.

I'VE SEEN MANY WOUNDS LIKE THAT IN MY VILLAGE. WE CALL THEM THE WALKING DEAD...

...BECAUSE IT TAKES ABOUT A WEEK FOR THE BARBS TO REACH THE VITAL ORGANS.

THAT ELECTROMAGNET IS KEEPING THE SHRAPNEL FROM ENTERING YOUR HEART.

...THE MOST *FAMOUS* MASS MURDERER IN THE HISTORY OF AMERICA.
I AM RAZA.
COME, NOW.

"THE BOW AND ARROW, MR. STARK, ONCE WAS THE *PINNACLE* OF WEAPONS TECHNOLOGY. IT ALLOWED THE GREAT *GENGHIS KHAN* TO RULE FROM THE PACIFIC TO THE UKRAINE...
"AN EMPIRE *TWICE* THE SIZE OF ALEXANDER THE GREAT'S. AND *FOUR TIMES* THE SIZE OF THE ROMAN EMPIRE."

BUT TODAY, WHOEVER HOLDS THE LATEST STARK WEAPONS RULES THESE LANDS. AND SOON... IT WILL BE *MY* TURN.
WE HAVE EVERYTHING YOU NEED IN TERMS OF RAW MATERIALS TO BUILD THE JERICHO MISSILE YOU DEMONSTRATED.
AND WHEN YOU HAVE DONE SO...

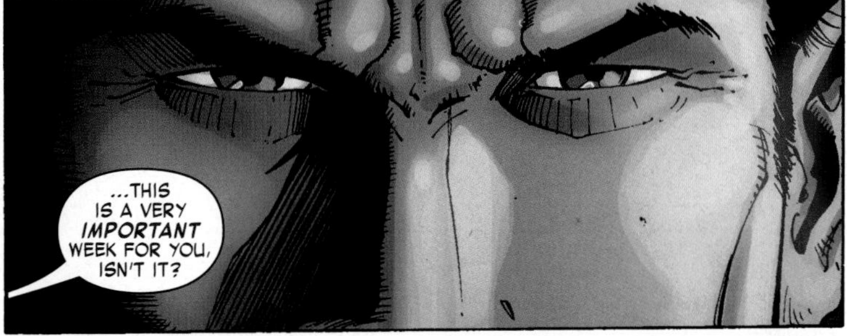

<WHAT IS HE DOING?>
<HE TOLD US HE NEEDED WELDING GEAR. A SOLDERING STATION, HELMETS, GOGGLES, PRECISION TOOLS...>
<AND NOW?>
<HE'S WORKING.>

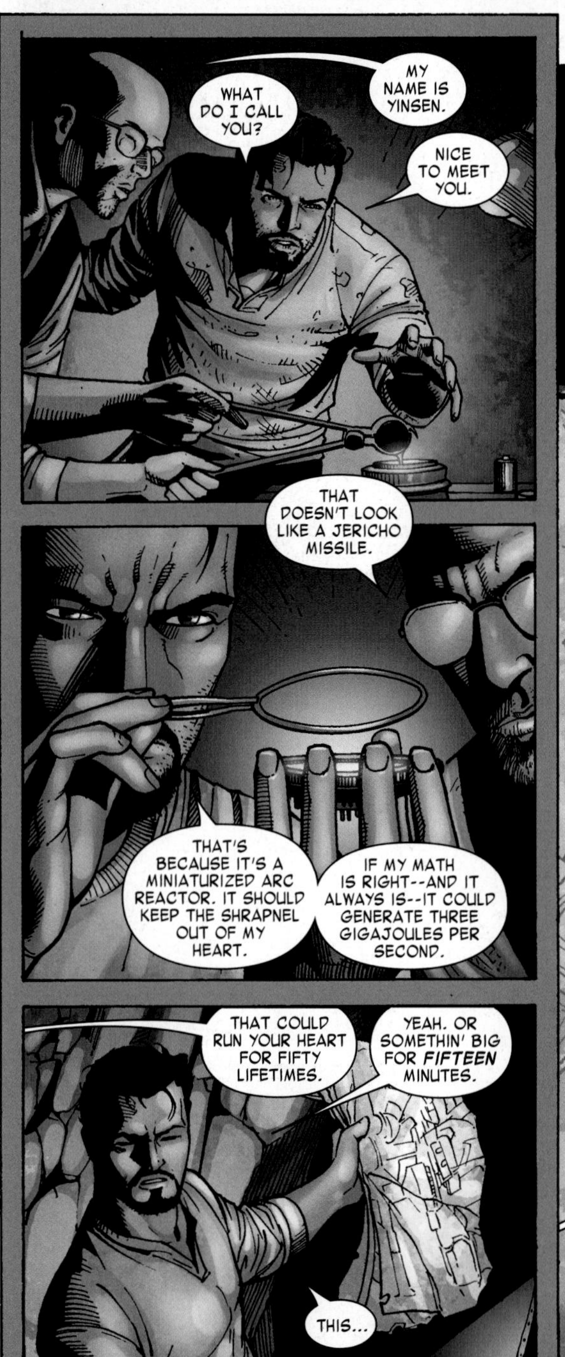

MY NAME IS YINSEN.
WHAT DO I CALL YOU?
NICE TO MEET YOU.
THAT DOESN'T LOOK LIKE A JERICHO MISSILE.
THAT'S BECAUSE IT'S A MINIATURIZED ARC REACTOR. IT SHOULD KEEP THE SHRAPNEL OUT OF MY HEART.
IF MY MATH IS RIGHT--AND IT ALWAYS IS--IT COULD GENERATE THREE GIGAJOULES PER SECOND.
THAT COULD RUN YOUR HEART FOR FIFTY LIFETIMES.
YEAH. OR SOMETHIN' BIG FOR *FIFTEEN* MINUTES.
THIS...
...IS OUR TICKET OUT OF HERE.

YOU STILL HAVEN'T TOLD ME WHERE YOU'RE FROM.
A SMALL TOWN CALLED GULMIRA. IT'S ACTUALLY A NICE PLACE.
GOT ANY FAMILY?
YES. AND I WILL SEE THEM WHEN I LEAVE HERE. AND *YOU*, STARK?
NO.
NO. HM. SO YOU'RE A MAN WHO HAS *EVERYTHING*... AND *NOTHING*.
WHY HAVE YOU FAILED ME, YINSEN? I LET YOU LIVE! *THIS* IS HOW YOU REPAY ME?
WE'RE WORKING DILIGENTLY! IT'S VERY COMPLEX! HE'S BUILDING YOUR JERICHO!
YOU HAVE UNTIL *TOMORROW*... TO ASSEMBLE MY MISSILE.

OKAY... OUR ESCAPE ROUTE AGAIN IS--?
FORTY STEPS STRAIGHT AHEAD...
THEN FORK RIGHT. THIRTY-THREE STEPS. TURN RIGHT.
YINSEN!

YINSEN! STARK!

BAKOOOM

WELL, THE EXPLOSIVES I RIGGED ON THE DOOR WORKED. NOW... INITIALIZE THE POWER SEQUENCE. FUNCTION ELEVEN.
TELL ME WHEN YOU SEE A PROGRESS BAR.

I HAVE IT.
PRESS CONTROL-I. THEN COME OVER HERE AND BUTTON ME UP.

THEY'RE COMING.
MAKE SURE THE CHECKPOINTS ARE CLEAR BEFORE YOU FOLLOW ME OUT, OKAY?
WE NEED MORE TIME.
I'M GOING TO BUY YOU SOME MORE TIME!
STICK TO THE PLAN!
YINSEN!
YAHHHHHHHH!
...
<THE REST OF YOU, KEEP GOING! FIND STARK!>

<YOU! WHAT ARE YOU DOING? THE LAB IS DOWN THAT WAY--!>
<STAY AWAY FROM THERE! IT WAS A MONSTER! A DEMON!>
<WHAT ARE YOU TALKING ABOUT YOU--?!>
KCHNK
EH--?
<I TOLD YOU! I-->
YINSEN!!

YINSEN!
W-WATCH OUT!
FWOOOOSH
BLAKOOOM
EEYARRHHHH!!

OME ON. E'VE GOT GO. WE GOT LAN. WE'RE NNA STICK TO IT.
THIS WAS *ALWAYS* THE PLAN, STARK.
YOU'RE GONNA GO SEE YOUR FAMILY. GET UP.
MY FAMILY IS DEAD. I'M GOING TO SEE THEM *NOW*, STARK.
It's okay. It's...
I want this. I want this...
THANK YOU FOR SAVING ME.
Don't waste it. Don't waste your life...

...unhhh...

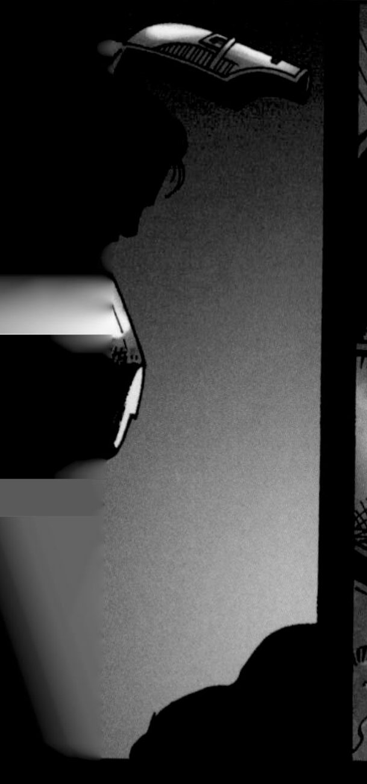

<HERE HE COMES! GE HIM!>

MY TURN.
FWOOOOOOSH

KLK
"COLONEL FURY! HOT CONTACT WEST OF THE KUNAR MOUNTAIN RANGE! SOME SORT OF NEW AIRCRAFT, EXCEPT..."
"EXCEPT WHAT, SITWELL?"

SITWELL, WHEN I SAY "EXCEPT WHAT," I EXPECT A RESPONSE.
IT'S JUST... IT'S TOO SMALL TO BE EVEN A ONE-MAN CRAFT. AND IT'S GOT AN ENERGY SIGNATURE LIKE I'VE NEVER SEEN BE--
UH-OH. CONTACT LOST.
"WHATEVER IT IS, IT MUST'VE CRASH-LANDED. MAYBE EVEN BROKE UP ON IMPACT."
"THAT CONTACT MAY BE THE FIRST SOLID LEAD TO STARK WE'VE GOTTEN, SITWELL. NOTIFY OUR FRIENDS IN THE D.O.D."
HUFF HUFFFFF
HEY!
HEY!
...RHODEY...
HOW WAS THE "FUN-VEE"?
HEH.
NEXT TIME, YOU RIDE WITH ME, OKAY?

EDWARDS AIR FORCE BASE...
YOUR EYES ARE RED, MISS POTTS. A FEW TEARS FOR YOUR LONG-LOST BOSS?
TEARS OF JOY. I HATE JOB HUNTING. TAKE US TO THE HOSPITAL, PLEASE, HAPPY.
ABSOLU--
NO.
NO?

I'VE BEEN IN CAPTIVITY FOR THREE MONTHS. THERE ARE TWO THINGS I WANT TO DO.
I WANT AN AMERICAN CHEESEBURGER. AND THE OTHER IS...
THAT'S ENOUGH OF *THAT*.
...NOT WHAT YOU THINK. I WANT YOU TO CALL A PRESS CONFERENCE.

"A PRESS CONFERENCE? WHAT ON EARTH FOR?"
ELCOME HOME TONY!
YOU *HAD* TO HAVE A BURGER?
YOU GET *ME* ONE OF THOSE?
ONLY ONE LEFT, OBADIAH. I NEED IT.

MISS POTTS, CAN I SPEAK TO YOU FOR A MOMENT?
I'M AGENT PHIL COULSON WITH THE STRATEGIC HOMELAND INTERVENTION ENFORCEMENT AND LOGISTICS DIVISION.
THAT'S QUITE A MOUTHFUL.
I KNOW. WE'RE WORKING ON IT.

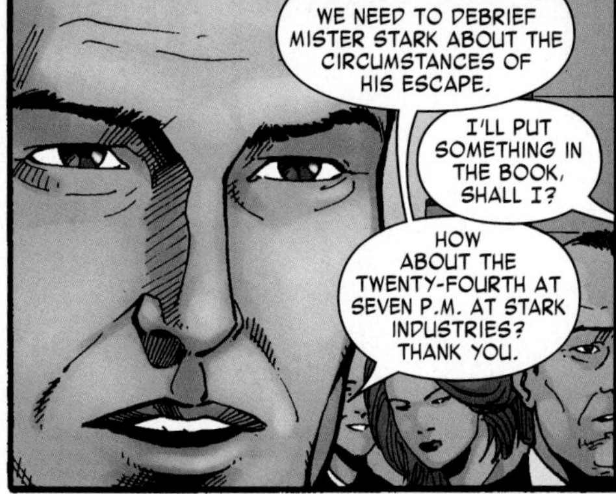
WE NEED TO DEBRIEF MISTER STARK ABOUT THE CIRCUMSTANCES OF HIS ESCAPE.
I'LL PUT SOMETHING IN THE BOOK, SHALL I?
HOW ABOUT THE TWENTY-FOURTH AT SEVEN P.M. AT STARK INDUSTRIES? THANK YOU.

MR. STARK, WHAT *HAPPENED* OVER THERE?
I SAW YOUNG AMERICANS KILLED BY THE VERY WEAPONS I CREATED TO DEFEND AND *PROTECT* THEM.
AND I SAW THAT I HAD BECOME PART OF A SYSTEM THAT IS COMFORTABLE WITH ZERO ACCOUNTABILITY.

I HAD MY EYES OPENED. I CAME TO REALIZE THAT I HAVE MORE TO OFFER THIS WORLD THAN JUST MAKING THINGS THAT BLOW UP. AND *THAT* IS WHY...
...I AM SHUTTING DOWN THE WEAPONS MANUFACTURING DIVISION OF STARK INTERNATIONAL.

MR. STARK!
OKAY, OKAY, *THANK YOU TONY!*
UNTIL SUCH A TIME AS I CAN DECIDE WHAT THE FUTURE OF HIS COMPANY WILL BE...
...WHAT *DIRECTION* IT SHOULD TAKE.
MR. STARK, OVER HERE!
WE'RE GONNA HAVE A LITTLE *INTERNAL* DISCUSSION.
...ONE THAT I'M *COMFORTABLE* WITH, AND IS CONSISTENT...

I THINK WE SHOULD TAKE ANOTHER LOOK INTO ARC REACTOR TECHNOLOGY.

TONY, *COME ON!* WE BUILT THAT THING TO SHUT THE HIPPIES UP! THE ARC WAS NEVER COST-EFFECTIVE. WE KNEW THAT BEFORE WE BUILT IT.

OH MY GOD. IS THAT THE THING THAT'S KEEPING YOU ALIVE?
IT WAS. IT IS NOW AN ANTIQUE. I WAS SWAPPING IT OUT FOR AN UPGRADED UNIT AND I JUST RAN INTO A LITTLE SNAG.
AN EXPOSED WIRE UNDER THIS DEVICE IS CONTACTING THE SOCKET WALL AND IT'S CAUSING A LITTLE BIT OF A SHORT.
PUT THAT ON THE TABLE OVER THERE.
OH MY GOD.
THEN YOU'RE JUST GONNA GENTLY LIFT THE WIRE OUT. I REALLY NEED YOUR HELP HERE.
ECCHHH! THERE'S PUS!
IT SMELLS!
IT'S NOT PUS! IT'S AN INORGANIC PLASMIC DISCHARGE. THAT'S FROM THE DEVICE, NOT FROM MY BODY.
YEAH, IT DOES. THE COPPER WIRE... YOU GOT IT?
I GOT IT.
NOW DON'T PULL OUT THE MAGNET AT THE END OF--
YOU PULLED IT OUT. OKAY. QUICKLY...
ATTACH THE NEW ONE TO THE BASE PLATE BEFORE I GO INTO CARDIAC ARREST.
THERE. ARE YOU OKAY?
YEAH. I FEEL GREAT.
DON'T EVER ASK ME TO DO ANYTHING LIKE THAT EVER AGAIN.
I DON'T HAVE ANYONE BUT YOU.
WHAT DO YOU WANT ME TO DO WITH THIS?
THAT? DESTROY IT. INCINERATE IT.
YOU DON'T WANT TO KEEP IT?
PEPPER, I'VE BEEN CALLED MANY THINGS-- NOSTALGIC IS NOT ONE OF THEM.

LOOK WHO FELL OUT OF THE SKY! MISTER TONY STARK.
I SWEAR, I DIDN'T EXPECT TO SEE YOU WALKIN' AROUND SO SOON.
I'M DOIN' A LITTLE BETTER THAN WALKING.

RHODEY, I'M WORKIN' ON SOMETHING BIG. I WANT YOU TO BE A PART OF IT.
YOU'RE ABOUT TO MAKE A WHOLE LOT OF PEOPLE AROUND HERE REAL HAPPY, 'CAUSE THAT LITTLE STUNT AT THE PRESS CONFERENCE...THAT WAS A DOOZY.

THIS IS NOT FOR THE MILITARY. I'M NOT...
IT'S DIFFERENT.
WHAT? YOU'RE A HUMANITARIAN NOW OR SOMETHIN'?
R'FORCE
I NEED YOU TO LISTEN TO ME.

NO.
WHAT YOU NEED IS TO GET YOUR MIND RIGHT.
HEH.
I'M SERIOUS.

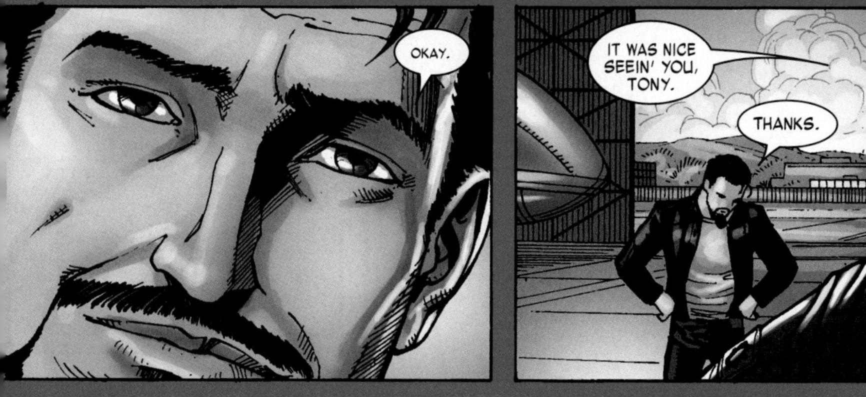
OKAY.
IT WAS NICE SEEIN' YOU, TONY.
THANKS.

"OKAY. LET'S DO THIS RIGHT."

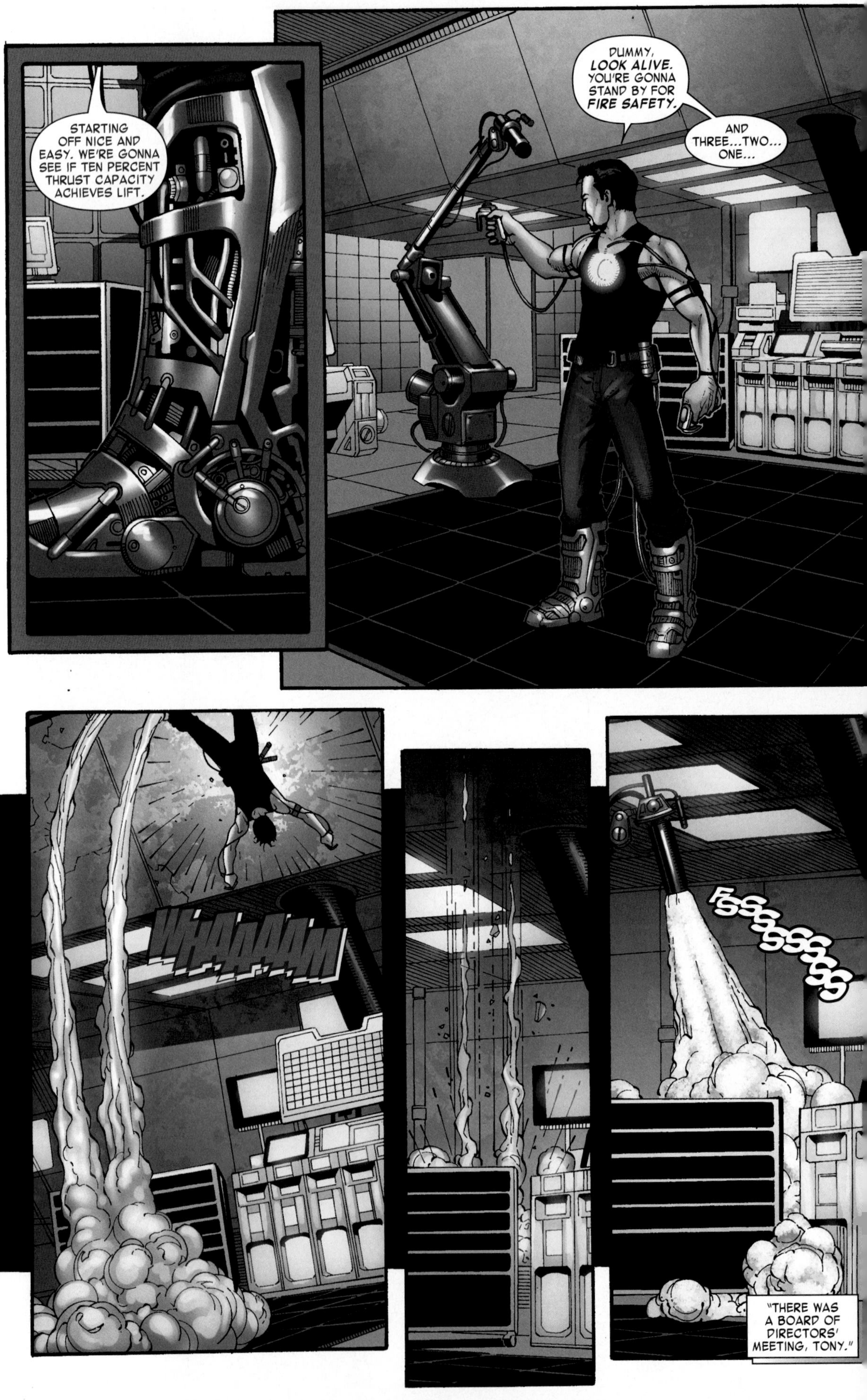

STARTING OFF NICE AND EASY. WE'RE GONNA SEE IF TEN PERCENT THRUST CAPACITY ACHIEVES LIFT.
DUMMY, **LOOK ALIVE.** YOU'RE GONNA STAND BY FOR ***FIRE SAFETY.***
AND THREE...TWO... ONE...

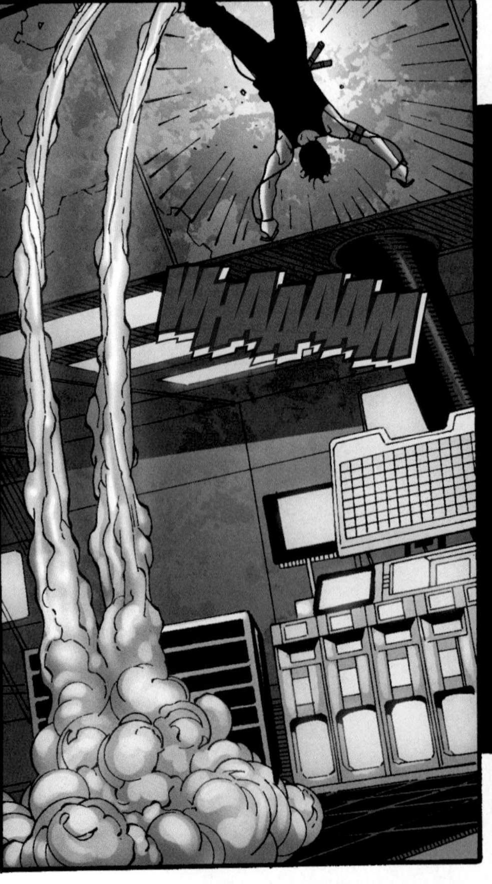

THEY'RE CLAIMING YOU HAVE POST-TRAUMATIC STRESS. THEY'RE FILING AN INJUNCTION. THEY WANT TO LOCK YOU OUT.
WHY? 'CAUSE THE STOCK'S DIPPED FORTY POINTS? WE KNEW THAT WAS GONNA HAPPEN.
FIFTY-SIX AND A HALF.

TONY, THE BOARD IS MAKING THE CASE THAT YOU AND YOUR NEW DIRECTION AREN'T IN THE COMPANY'S BEST INTERESTS!
I'M BEING RESPONSIBLE! THAT'S A NEW DIRECTION...FOR ME, FOR THE COMPANY.
I'M TRYING TO TURN THIS THING AROUND, BUT YOU'VE GOT TO GIVE ME SOMETHING TO PITCH 'EM.

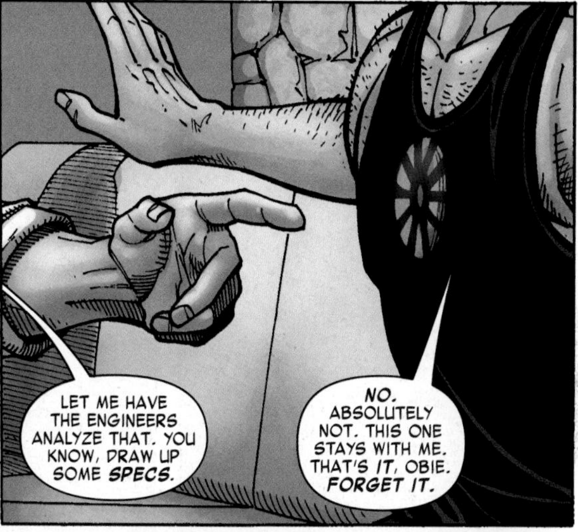
LET ME HAVE THE ENGINEERS ANALYZE THAT. YOU KNOW, DRAW UP SOME SPECS.
NO. ABSOLUTELY NOT. THIS ONE STAYS WITH ME. THAT'S IT, OBIE. FORGET IT.

WELL, DO YOU MIND IF I COME DOWN TO THE WORKSHOP AND SEE WHAT YOU'RE DOIN'?
GOOD NIGHT, OBIE.

DAY ELEVEN, TEST THIRTY-SEVEN. FOR LACK OF A BETTER OPTION, DUMMY IS STILL ON FIRE SAFETY.
IF YOU DOUSE ME AGAIN, AND I'M NOT ON FIRE, I'M DONATING YOU TO A CITY COLLEGE.
ALL RIGHT, NICE AND EASY. ONE PERCENT THRUST CAPACITY. AND THREE, TWO, ONE...

OKAY. LET'S BRING IT UP TO TWO-POINT-FIVE.

THERE IT IS. OKAY... EASY...
OKAY, THIS IS WHERE I DON'T WANNA BE!
NOT THE CARS! NOT THE--
--CARS!
COULD'VE GONE WORSE! COULD BE WORSE! WE'RE FINE!
OKAY! WE'RE GETTING THERE! AH-AH-AH-AH...
YEAH. I CAN FLY.

J.A.R.V.I.S., IMPORT ALL PREFERENCES FROM HOME INTERFACE.
WILL DO, SIR.
DO A CHECK ON CONTROL SURFACES.
AS YOU WISH.
MARK TWO TEST COMPLETE. PREPARING TO POWER DOWN AND BEGIN DIAGNOSTICS.
UH, YEAH. TELL YOU WHAT. DO A WEATHER AND A.T.C. CHECK. START LISTENING IN ON GROUND CONTROL.
SIR, THERE ARE STILL TERABYTES OF CALCULATIONS NEEDED BEFORE AN ACTUAL FLIGHT IS ATTEMPTED.
J.A.R.V.I.S., SOMETIMES YOU GOTTA RUN BEFORE YOU CAN WALK.
READY? IN THREE... TWO...

YEEEEEAAAHHHH!!!
HANDLES LIKE A DREAM!
ALL RIGHT, LET'S SEE WHAT THIS THING CAN DO. WHAT'S THE SR-71'S RECORD?
THE ALTITUDE RECORD FOR FIXED-WING FLIGHT IS EIGHTY-FIVE THOUSAND FEET, SIR.
RECORDS ARE MADE TO BE BROKEN!
SIR, THERE IS A POTENTIALLY FATAL BUILD-UP OF ICE OCCURRING.
KEEP GOIN'! HIGHER!

UH...
J.A.R.V.I.S.! WE ICED UP! DEPLOY FLAPS!
J.A.R.V.I.S.! COME ON, WE GOTTA BREAK THE ICE!
ARRRRRHHH!!!
DEPLOY FLAPS! DEPLOY--!
YEAH! AHAAAAHAHAAA!
OKAY. KILL POWER.

KRUUUNK
KRUUUNK
KRUUUNK
KRAAASH
FSSSSSSSSS

From Pepper
CONNECT TO THE CISCO. HAVE IT RECONFIGURE THE SHELL METALS.

USE THE GOLD TITANIUM ALLOY FROM THE SERAPHIM TACTICAL SATELLITE. THAT SHOULD ENSURE FUSELAGE INTEGRITY WHILE MAINTAINING POWER-TO-WEIGHT RATIO. GOT IT?
YES. SHALL I RENDER USING PROPOSED SPECIFICATIONS?

THRILL ME.
PROOF THAT TONY STARK HAS A HEART.

TONIGHT'S RED-HOT RED CARPET IS RIGHT HERE AT THE DISNEY CONCERT HALL, WHERE TONY STARK'S THIRD ANNUAL BENEFIT FOR THE FIREFIGHTERS' FAMILY FUND...
...HAS BECOME THE PLACE TO BE FOR L.A.'S HIGH SOCIETY.
ZORIANNA KIT
10

J.A.R.V.I.S., WE GET AN INVITE FOR THAT?
I HAVE NO RECORD OF AN INVITATION, SIR.
OUR VERY OWN HOST OF THE EVENING HASN'T BEEN SEEN IN PUBLIC SINCE HIS BIZARRE AND HIGHLY CONTROVERSIAL PRESS CONFERENCE.

SOME CLAIM HE'S SUFFERING FROM POST-TRAUMATIC STRESS AND HAS BEEN BED-RIDDEN FOR WEEKS. WHATEVER THE CASE, NO ONE EXPECTS AN APPEARANCE FROM TONY STARK TONIGHT.
THE RENDER IS COMPLETE.

STARK 4

"COMMENCING AUTOMATED ASSEMBLY. ESTIMATED COMPLETION TIME IS FIVE HOURS."

"MM-HMM.

MRK3 V02

"DON'T WAIT UP FOR ME, HONEY."

MR. STARK, LOOK OVER HERE!
HERE!
TONY, REMEMBER ME?
SURE DON'T.
CTV
TONY, LOOK THIS WAY!
LOOK WHO'S HERE...

MS. POTTS, YOU LOOK FANTASTIC. I DIDN'T RECOGNIZE YOU. HEY, WHERE'D YOU GET THAT DRESS?
OH, IT WAS A BIRTHDAY PRESENT... FROM YOU, ACTUALLY.
WELL, I'VE GOT GREAT TASTE. YOU WANT TO DANCE?
OH, NO. NO, THANK YOU, NO.
ALL RIGHT.
AM I MAKING YOU UNCOMFORTABLE?
OH, NO. NO, I ALWAYS FORGET TO WEAR DEODORANT AND DANCE WITH MY BOSS IN FRONT OF EVERYONE THAT I WORK WITH IN A DRESS WITH NO BACK.
UHM... LET'S GET SOME AIR.
THAT WAS TOTALLY WEIRD.
WE JUST DANCED.
NO, IT WAS NOT JUST A DANCE. LOOK, EVERYBODY KNOWS WHO YOU ARE AND HOW YOU ARE WITH GIRLS...BUT YOU'RE MY BOSS AND...
WOULD YOU LIKE A DRINK?
I WOULD. VODKA MARTINI, WITH OLIVES, LOTS OF OLIVES.

HI. TWO VODKA MARTINIS, EXTRA DRY, EXTRA OLIVES, EXTRA FAST.
WOW. TONY STARK. FANCY SEEING YOU HERE.

CARRIE.
CHRISTINE.
THAT'S RIGHT.
YOU HAVE A LOT OF NERVE SHOWING UP TONIGHT. CAN I AT LEAST GET A REACTION FROM YOU?

PANIC. I WOULD SAY PANIC IS MY REACTION.
I WAS REFERRING TO YOUR COMPANY'S INVOLVEMENT IN THIS LATEST ATROCITY.
YEAH, THEY JUST PUT MY NAME ON THE INVITATION. I DON'T KNOW WHAT TO TELL YA.

I'M SERIOUS. IS THIS WHAT YOU CALL ACCOUNTABILITY? IT'S A TOWN CALLED GULMIRA.

WHEN WERE THESE TAKEN?
YESTERDAY.
I DIDN'T APPROVE ANY SHIPMENT.
WELL, YOUR COMPANY DID.
STARK INDUSTRIES

WELL, I'M NOT MY COMPANY.

OBADIAH, HAVE YOU SEEN THESE PICTURES? HUH? WHAT'S GOING ON IN GULMIRA?
ARE WE DOUBLE-DEALING UNDER THE TABLE? ARE WE?
LET'S TAKE A PICTURE. COME ON. PICTURE TIME!
OBIE--
WHO DO YOU THINK LOCKED YOU OUT OF THE COMPANY? I WAS THE ONE WHO FILED THE INJUNCTION AGAINST YOU.
IT WAS THE ONLY WAY I COULD PROTECT YOU.
"THE FIFTEEN-MILE HIKE TO THE OUTSKIRTS OF GULMIRA CAN ONLY BE DESCRIBED AS A DESCENT INTO HELL, INTO A MODERN-DAY HEART OF DARKNESS."

SIMPLE FARMERS AND HERDERS FROM PEACEFUL VILLAGES HAVE BEEN DRIVEN FROM THEIR HOMES, DISPLACED FROM THEIR LANDS BY WARLORDS EMBOLDENED BY A NEWFOUND POWER.

CCN

RECENT VIOLENCE HAS BEEN ATTRIBUTED TO A GROUP OF FOREIGN FIGHTERS REFERRED TO BY LOCALS AS THE **TEN RINGS**.

THERE'S VERY **LITTLE** HOPE FOR THESE REFUGEES...

...WE CAN ONLY WONDER WHO, IF ANYONE...

FWZAAAAAM

...WILL **HELP**.

GULMIRA...

R-BLAM
OOOOF!
BOOM
FWEE
FOOOF
TINK
KATHOOOM

EDWARDS AIR FORCE BASE...
HELLO?
TONY? IT'S RHODES!
SPEAK UP PLEASE.
NINTH AIR FORCE
WHAT IN THE HELL IS THAT NOISE?
I'M DRIVING WITH THE TOP DOWN.
THERE WAS A WEAPONS DEPOT THAT WAS JUST BLOWN UP A FEW CLICKS FROM WHERE YOU WERE BEIN' HELD CAPTIVE.
YOU HAVE ANY TECH IN THE AREA I SHOULD KNOW ABOUT?
NOPE.
GOOD...
'CAUSE I'M STARING AT ONE ON RADAR RIGHT NOW, AND IT'S ABOUT TO BE BLOWN TO KINGDOM COME.
UH...THAT'S MY EXIT. GOTTA GO.
"COLONEL FURY! ANOTHER BOGEY WITH AN ENERGY SIGNATURE SIMILAR TO THE ONE FROM KABUL!"
HOW SIMILAR? HOW IS IT DIFFERENT?
IT'S STRONGER. AND IT'S FASTER. A LOT FASTER.
AND TWO F-22 RAPTORS HAVE JUST GONE WEAPONS HOT.
SEND WORD TO EDWARDS. HAVE THEM CALL 'EM OFF.
TOO LATE, COLONEL. THEY ATTEMPTED RADIO CONTACT AND GOT NO RESPONSE.

"THEY'VE ENGAGED THE BOGEY."
FOOOM
"THIS IS WHIPLASH ONE! BOGEY DEPLOYED FLARES AGAINST MISSILES!"
KSHOOOM
LOST VISUAL!
HI, RHODEY? IT'S ME. WHAT YOU WERE ASKING ABOUT IS ME.
THIS ISN'T A GAME! YOU DO NOT SEND CIVILIAN EQUIPMENT INTO MY ACTIVE WAR ZONE! YOU UNDERSTAND THAT?
THIS IS NOT A PIECE OF EQUIPMENT! I'M IN IT! IT'S A SUIT! IT'S ME!

WHIPLASH TWO--ON YOUR BELLY! IT LOOKS LIKE A...MAN!
SHAKE HIM OFF! ROLL!

OOOOOF!

I'M HIT! I'M HIT!

WHIPLASH ONE DOWN!
NINTH AIR FORCE
WHIPLASH TWO, DO YOU SEE A CHUTE?
NEGATIVE! NO CHUTE, NO CHUTE!

MY CHUTE'S JAMMED!

MY CHUTE'S--
KRNCH
FWOOOOMMFF

GOOD CHUTE! GOOD CHUTE!

TONY? OH MY GOD, YOU **CRAZY** SON OF A--
YOU OWE ME A PLANE. YOU KNOW THAT, RIGHT?
YEAH, WELL TECHNICALLY, HE HIT **ME**, SO...
NOW ARE YOU GONNA COME BY AND SEE WHAT I'M WORKING ON?

NO. THE LESS I KNOW, THE BETTER. NOW WHAT AM I SUPPOSED TO TELL THE PRESS?
UH, TRAINING EXERCISE? ISN'T THAT THE **USUAL** B.S.?
IT'S NOT THAT SIMPLE.

AN UNFORTUNATE TRAINING EXERCISE INVOLVING AN F-22 RAPTOR OCCURRED YESTERDAY. THE PILOT WAS NOT INJURED.

AS FOR THE UNEXPECTED TURN OF EVENTS ON THE GROUND IN GULMIRA...
OW! BE GENTLE! THIS IS MY FIRST TIME.
I DESIGNED THIS TO COME OFF, SO... AHHHHH!

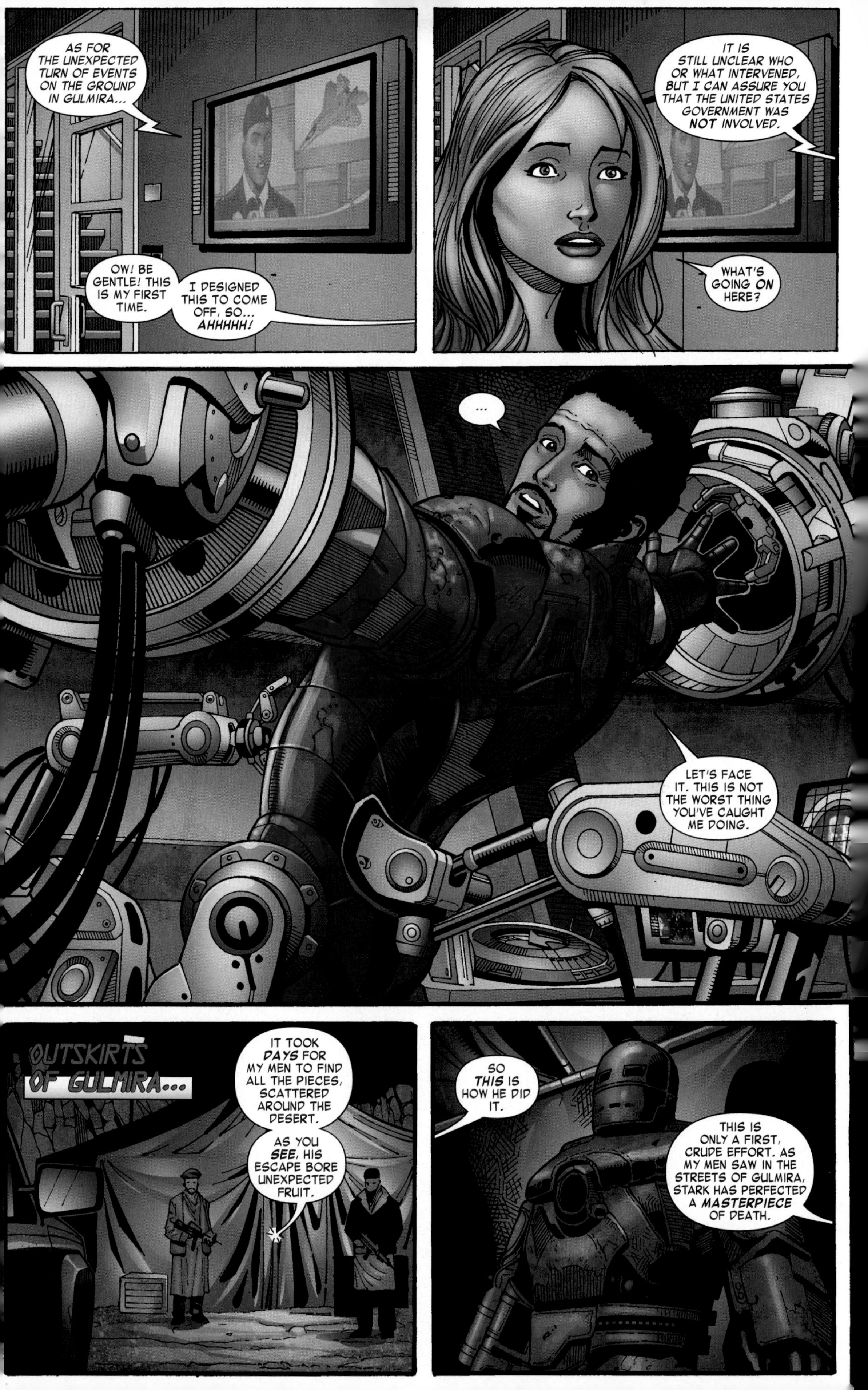

IT IS STILL UNCLEAR WHO OR WHAT INTERVENED, BUT I CAN ASSURE YOU THAT THE UNITED STATES GOVERNMENT WAS NOT INVOLVED.
WHAT'S GOING ON HERE?

...
LET'S FACE IT. THIS IS NOT THE WORST THING YOU'VE CAUGHT ME DOING.

OUTSKIRTS OF GULMIRA...
IT TOOK DAYS FOR MY MEN TO FIND ALL THE PIECES, SCATTERED AROUND THE DESERT.
AS YOU SEE, HIS ESCAPE BORE UNEXPECTED FRUIT.

SO THIS IS HOW HE DID IT.
THIS IS ONLY A FIRST, CRUDE EFFORT. AS MY MEN SAW IN THE STREETS OF GULMIRA, STARK HAS PERFECTED A MASTERPIECE OF DEATH.

A MAN WITH A DOZEN OF THESE CAN RULE ALL OF ASIA.

AND YOU DREAM OF STARK'S THRONE. WE HAVE A COMMON ENEMY.
IF WE ARE STILL IN BUSINESS, I WILL GIVE YOU THESE DESIGNS AS A GIFT. AND IN TURN...
I HOPE YOU'LL REPAY ME WITH A GIFT OF IRON SOLDIERS.

ZZZZT
NNNHH--
THIS IS THE ONLY GIFT YOU SHALL RECEIVE.
DON'T WORRY. THE PARALYSIS ONLY LASTS FIFTEEN MINUTES. THAT'S THE LEAST OF YOUR PROBLEMS.

CRATE UP THE ARMOR. LET'S FINISH UP HERE.

BLAM
BLAM
SET UP SECTOR SIXTEEN, UNDERNEATH THE ARC REACTOR. RECRUIT OUR TOP ENGINEERS. I WANT A PROTOTYPE RIGHT AWAY.

PEPPER, I NEED YOU TO GO TO MY OFFICE, HACK INTO THE MAINFRAME, AND RETRIEVE ALL THE RECENT SHIPPING MANIFESTS.
THEY'VE BEEN DEALING UNDER THE TABLE AND I'M GONNA STOP 'EM. I'M GONNA FIND MY WEAPONS AND DESTROY THEM.
TONY, I CANNOT HELP YOU IF YOU'RE GONNA START ALL OF THIS AGAIN.
THERE IS NOTHING EXCEPT THIS. THERE'S NO ART OPENING, NO BENEFIT, NOTHING TO SIGN. THERE'S THE NEXT MISSION AND NOTHING ELSE.
THEN I QUIT.
YOU STOOD BY MY SIDE ALL THESE YEARS WHILE I REAPED THE BENEFITS OF DESTRUCTION...
AND NOW THAT I'M TRYING TO PROTECT THE PEOPLE THAT I PUT IN HARM'S WAY, YOU'RE GONNA WALK OUT?
YOU'RE GONNA KILL YOURSELF, TONY. I'M NOT GONNA BE A PART OF IT.
"PEPPER...I SHOULDN'T BE ALIVE UNLESS IT WAS FOR A REASON.
"I JUST FINALLY KNOW WHAT I HAVE TO DO. AND I KNOW IN MY HEART THAT IT'S RIGHT."
"SIGH TONY...YOU'RE ALL I HAVE TOO, YOU KNOW."

YOU DID NOT TELL US THAT THE TARGET YOU PAID US TO KILL WAS THE GREAT TONY STARK.
GHOST DRIVE FOUND
Sector 16 Files
OH MY GOD.
AS YOU CAN SEE, OBADIAH STANE...
YOUR DECEPTION AND LIES WILL COST YOU DEARLY. THE PRICE TO KILL TONY STARK HAS JUST GONE UP.
DOWNLOAD COMPLETE
I KNOW WHAT YOU'RE GOING THROUGH.
I WAS SO HAPPY WHEN HE CAME HOME. IT WAS LIKE WE GOT HIM BACK FROM THE DEAD. AND NOW I REALIZE... WELL...
TONY NEVER REALLY DID COME HOME. HE LEFT A PART OF HIMSELF IN THAT CAVE.

YOU'RE A VERY RARE WOMAN.
THANKS. I'D...BETTER GET BACK TO TONY.

100
DOWNLOAD COMPLETE
"MS. POTTS? AGENT COULSON. DID YOU FORGET ABOUT OUR APPOINTMENT?"

NOPE, RIGHT NOW. COME WITH ME.
RIGHT NOW?
YUP. WALK WITH ME...

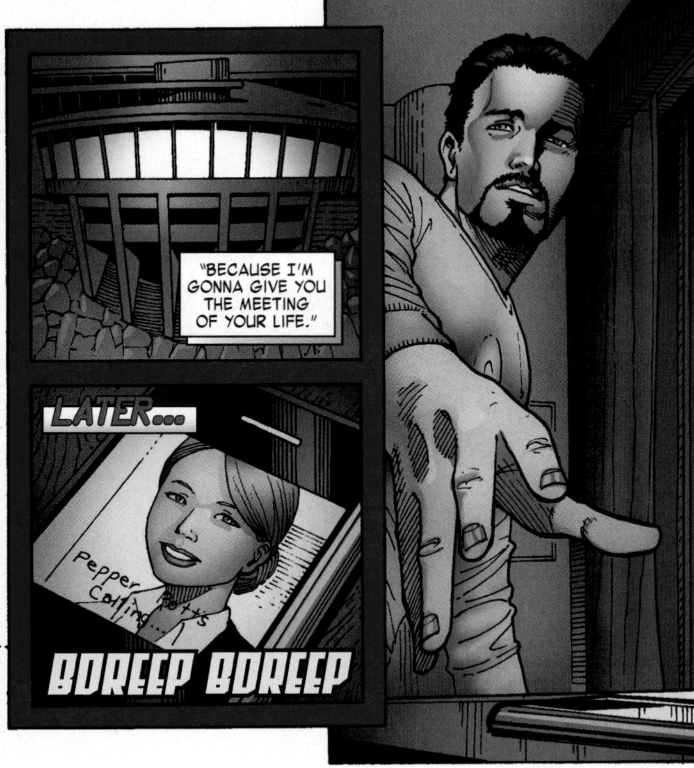
"BECAUSE I'M GONNA GIVE YOU THE MEETING OF YOUR LIFE."
LATER...
Pepper Potts Calling...
BDREEP BDREEP

WHEN I ORDERED THE HIT ON YOU, I WORRIED THAT I WAS *KILLING* THE GOLDEN GOOSE. BUT YOU SEE, IT WAS JUST FATE THAT YOU SURVIVED THAT.

YOU HAD ONE LAST GOLDEN EGG TO GIVE.

THIS IS YOUR LEGACY. A NEW GENERATION OF WEAPONS WITH *THIS* AT ITS HEART.

WEAPONS THAT WILL HELP STEER THE WORLD BACK ON COURSE...PUT THE BALANCE OF POWER IN OUR HANDS. THE *RIGHT* HANDS.

TOO BAD YOU HAD TO INVOLVE PEPPER IN THIS.

TONY! TONY, YOU OKAY?
HAS A HEART
STARK
I AM NOW. WHERE'S PEPPER?
SHE'S FINE. SHE'S WITH FIVE AGENTS. THEY'RE ABOUT TO ARREST OBADIAH AT SECTOR SIXTEEN.
THEY'RE NOT GONNA BE ENOUGH.
THAT'S THE COOLEST THING I'VE EVER SEEN.
NOT BAD, HUH? LET'S DO IT.
YOU NEED ME TO DO ANYTHING ELSE?
KEEP THE SKIES CLEAR.
DAMN.
NEXT TIME, BABY.

SECTOR 16...
LOOKS LIKE YOU WERE RIGHT, MS. POTTS. STANE WAS BUILDING A SUIT.

I THOUGHT IT WOULD BE BIGGER.

EEEEEEEEEE!!!
TAKE HIM OUT!!
BLAM BLAM
WHERE DO YOU THINK YOU'RE GOING?

PEPPER?!
TONY! O-OBADIAH... HE'S GONE INSANE! HE BUILT A SUIT! HE--
YOUR SERVICES ARE NO LONGER REQUIRED.
AAAAAAA--!
STAAAAAANE!

COLLATERAL DAMAGE, TONY!

PUT 'EM DOWN!

J.A.R.V.I.S.! DIVERT POWER TO REPULSORS!

UNHHH!!!
I BUILT THIS COMPANY FROM NOTHING!
AND NO ONE IS GOING TO STAND IN MY WAY!

THIRTEEN PERCENT POWER, SIR.
CLIMB!
ELEVEN PERCENT.
KEEP GOIN'!
SEVEN PERCENT POWER--
STOP TELLIN' ME!

YOU HAD A GREAT IDEA, TONY. BUT MY SUIT IS MORE ADVANCED IN EVERY WAY!
HOW'D YOU SOLVE THE ICING PROBLEM?

ICING... PROBLEM...?

MIGHT WANT TO LOOK INTO IT!
WE ARE NOW RUNNING ON EMERGENCY BACKUP POWER.

WHOAAAAA!

POTTS!
TONY! OH MY GOD, ARE YOU OKAY?

I MANAGED TO LAND ON THE ROOF OF THE GENERATOR BUILDING, BUT I'M ALMOST OUT OF POWER. I'VE GOT TO GET OUT OF THIS THING.

NICE TRY!

REPULSORS OFFLINE. MISSILES OFFLINE.
FLARES!

ARRRHHH!
FWOOOOF

POTTS! THIS ISN'T WORKING. WE'RE GONNA HAVE TO OVERLOAD THE REACTOR AND BLAST THE ROOF.
WELL, HOW ARE YOU GONNA DO THAT?
YOU'RE GONNA DO IT.

GO TO THE CENTRAL CONSOLE, OPEN UP ALL THE CIRCUITS.
WHEN I GET CLEAR OF THE ROOF, I'LL LET YOU KNOW. YOU'RE GONNA HIT THE MASTER BYPASS BUTTON. IT'LL FRY EVERYTHING UP HERE.

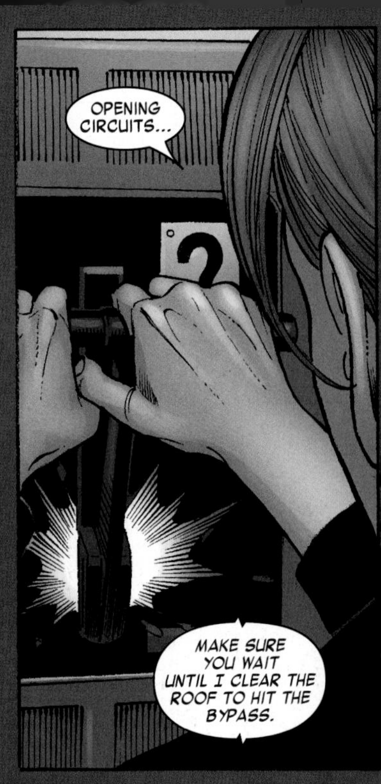
OPENING CIRCUITS...
MAKE SURE YOU WAIT UNTIL I CLEAR THE ROOF TO HIT THE BYPASS.

I'LL BUY YOU SOME TIME.
THIS LOOKS IMPORTANT!
SHOULD TAKE OUT ALL YOUR OPTICALS.

I NEVER HAD A TASTE FOR THIS SORT OF THING...
BUT I MUST ADMIT--
I'M DEEPLY ENJOYING THE SUIT!
KRNCH
IT'S READY, TONY! GET OFF THE ROOF!
HOW IRONIC, TONY!
BUDDA BUDDA BUDDA

IN TRYING TO RID THE WORLD OF WEAPONS--
YOU GAVE IT ITS BEST ONE EVER!
AND NOW I'M GONNA KILL YOU WITH IT!
PEPPER! TIME TO HIT THE BUTTON!
PUSH IT!
YOU TOLD ME NOT TO! YOU'LL DIE!
KLIK

"YOU'VE ALL RECEIVED THE OFFICIAL STATEMENT.
"A ROBOTIC PROTOTYPE MALFUNCTIONED AND CAUSED DAMAGE TO THE ARC REACTOR."

FORTUNATELY A MEMBER OF TONY STARK'S PERSONAL SECURITY STAFF WAS ABLE TO NEUTRALIZE THAT SITUATION.
6
10

"IRON MAN." NOT TECHNICALLY ACCURATE. THE SUIT'S A GOLD/TITANIUM ALLOY, BUT IT'S KIND OF EVOCATIVE.
HERE'S YOUR ALIBI. WE HAVE PORT PAPERS THAT PUT YOU IN AVALON ALL NIGHT. JUST READ THE CARDS WORD FOR WORD.
The Chronicle
WHO IS THE IRON MAN?

THERE'S NOTHING ABOUT STANE HERE, COULSON.
HE'S ON VACATION. SMALL AIRCRAFT HAVE SUCH A POOR SAFETY RECORD.

YOU'LL BE HEARING FROM US.
FROM THE STRATEGIC HOMELAND INT--?
JUST CALL US S.H.I.E.L.D.

YOU KNOW... IF I WERE IRON MAN, I'D HAVE THIS GIRLFRIEND WHO KNEW MY TRUE IDENTITY. SHE'D BE WILDLY CONFLICTED, WHICH WOULD ONLY MAKE HER MORE CRAZY ABOUT ME.
TELL ME YOU NEVER THINK ABOUT THAT NIGHT.

THAT NIGHT WE DANCED, AND THEN YOU WENT DOWNSTAIRS TO GET ME A DRINK...
AND YOU LEFT ME THERE, BY MYSELF?
MMMHHM.

WILL THAT BE ALL, MISTER STARK?
THAT WILL BE ALL, MISS POTTS.

UH...BEEN A WHILE SINCE I WAS IN FRONT OF YOU. I FIGURE I'LL STICK TO THE CARDS THIS TIME.
THERE'S BEEN SPECULATION THAT I WAS INVOLVED IN THE EVENTS THAT--
I'M SORRY, MISTER STARK...

BUT DO YOU HONESTLY EXPECT US TO BELIEVE THAT WAS A BODYGUARD IN A SUIT THAT CONVENIENTLY APPEARED--?

I KNOW THAT IT'S CONFUSING, BUT CLEARLY, I'M NOT THE HERO TYPE, WITH MY LAUNDRY LIST OF CHARACTER DEFECTS...
JUST STICK TO THE CARDS, MAN.
YEAH, OKAY. YEAH. THE TRUTH IS...

I AM IRON MAN.

THAT NIGHT...
"I AM IRON MAN." YOU THINK YOU'RE THE ONLY SUPER HERO IN THE WORLD?

HUH? HOW DID YOU GET IN HERE?
WHO THE HELL ARE YOU?
MISTER STARK, YOU'VE BECOME PART OF A BIGGER UNIVERSE. YOU JUST DON'T KNOW IT YET.
NICK FURY. DIRECTOR OF S.H.I.E.L.D.
I'M HERE TO TALK TO YOU ABOUT THE AVENGERS INITIATIVE.

OPPORTUNITIES AREN'T OFFERED. THEY'RE TAKEN. IF THERE'S ONE OUT THERE, I'LL FIND IT MYSELF.
I DON'T NEED GOVERNMENT INTRUDERS IN MY HOUSE DANGLING THEM.
YOU KNOW THE WAY OUT, MR. FURRY.
FURY. AND I'LL BE KEEPING AN EYE ON YOU, STARK.
WELL, YOU'VE JUST GOT THE ONE, SO TRY NOT TO TRIP OVER ANYTHING.
COULSON. THIS IS FURY. LOOKS LIKE YOU HAD OUR BOY PEGGED.
SO HE'S A NO-GO, COLONEL?
OH, HE'LL GO. HE JUST NEEDS THE RIGHT APPROACH.
INFORM NATASHA WE'LL BE NEEDING HER SERVICES...

RON MAN: PUBLIC IDENTITY #1
COVER BY ADI GRANOV

...YOU'VE ALL RECEIVED THE OFFICIAL STATEMENT OF WHAT OCCURRED AT STARK INDUSTRIES LAST NIGHT...
HERE'S YOUR ALIBI.
YOU WERE ON YOUR YACHT. WE HAVE PORT PAPERS THAT PUT YOU IN AVALON ALL NIGHT AND SWORN STATEMENTS FROM FIFTY OF YOUR GUESTS...
WHAT ABOUT THE WHOLE COVER STORY THAT IT'S... A BODYGUARD?
THAT'S KINDA FLIMSY, COULSON, DON'TCHA THINK?
The Chronicle
WHO IS THE IRON MAN?
OL. JAMES RHODES
AND NOW MISTER STARK HAS PREPARED A STATEMENT...
THANKS, RHODEY.
...
I AM IRON MAN.

DECADES AGO
YOUR ENGLISH IS GETTING BETTER, ANTON.
PERHAPS. WHETHER OR NOT THIS "UNITY PROJECT" OF YOURS WILL BEAR FRUIT IS ANOTHER MATTER ENTIRELY...
...CONSIDERING THE POSTURING OF OUR NATIONS' GOVERNMENTS.
FORGET ABOUT THEM. MY MILITARY CONTRACTS ARE MERELY THE SHORTEST DISTANCE BETWEEN TWO POINTS. THINK ABOUT THE CHILDREN WE'LL BOTH HAVE SOMEDAY...
...THAT'S OUR PRIORITY.
THANK YOU, JARVIS.
THE POINT IS... IF I WANT YOU ON MY TEAM, YOU'RE ON MY TEAM. NO QUESTIONS ASKED. I'VE EARNED THAT.
VERY WELL, HOWARD.
AS ALWAYS, I AM HUMBLED BY YOUR TRUST.
AND YET, I MUST EXPRESS MY CONTINUED CONCERNS...
...THIS ARC REACTOR TECHNOLOGY. THE IMPLICATIONS ALONE OF SUCH A DEVICE EVEN EXISTING...
...HAVE YOU NOT THOUGHT ABOUT THESE THINGS?
THEY SAID THE SAME THING ABOUT THE MANHATTAN PROJECT...
DIDN'T THEY, MARIA...?
"WHERE IGNORANCE IS BLISS..."
"...'TIS FOLLY TO BE WISE."

SO SPEAKS THE GREAT HOWARD STARK. YOUR CAVALIER ATTITUDE MAY WORK FOR THE PRESS.
BUT TO APPROACH SCIENCE IN SUCH A MANNER, IT'S...
...UNSEEMLY.
THAT'S HOW SCIENCE WORKS IN THIS COUNTRY. THINK ABOUT IT. THE ANCILLARY APPLICATIONS ALONE JUSTIFY THE EXPERIMENT.
BUT PERHAPS NOT THE EXPENSE...
SINCE WHEN ARE YOU AN ACCOUNTANT? WE'RE ABOUT TO EMBARK ON DEVELOPING TECHNOLOGY THAT'S GOING TO CHANGE THE WORLD AND YOU'RE TALKING DOLLARS AND CENTS.
I'M AN INVENTOR. I DREAM BIG AND THEN I DO WHATEVER IT TAKES TO MAKE THOSE DREAMS A REALITY.
NOW YOU'VE SEEN THE SCHEMATICS. YOU KNOW IT CAN WORK.
DON'T WORRY ABOUT THE POLITICS INVOLVED. THIS IS MUCH BIGGER THAN THAT.
WE'RE SERVING A GLOBAL COMMUNITY THAT DOESN'T EVEN RECOGNIZE ITS OWN EXISTENCE.
I'VE PLAYED THE GAME FOR YEARS, ANTON. SO HAVE YOU.
IT'S TIME TO CHANGE THE GAME.
WE DON'T HAVE TO WALK THAT PATH THAT LEADS TOWARD MUTUALLY ASSURED DESTRUCTION...
...THERE'S ANOTHER FUTURE OUT THERE WAITING FOR US.

TODAY.
HEY, GIRLS--
--NOW THIS IS A PRACTICAL APPLICATION OF TECHNOLOGY!

THERE HE IS!
YOU MISSED IT, HAPPY. IT WAS LIKE...A SCHOOL FIELD TRIP.
EXTREMELY EDUCATIONAL.
I'M SURE IT WAS, SIR.
SORRY, BOYS...I'M OFF DUTY TONIGHT.
DON'T WORRY. I'LL BE SAVING THE WORLD AGAIN TOMORROW, I'M SURE.
LADIES.
LATER ON WE'LL HIT THE GROTTO AND I'LL SHOW SOME OF YOU EXACTLY WHY THEY CALL ME "IRON MAN..."
IS THAT COOL, HEF?
IT'S YOUR WORLD, TONY. WE'RE JUST LIVING IN IT.
...HE'S THE FIRST CELEBRITY SUPER HERO AND WE CAN'T GET ENOUGH OF HIM!
WHEN HE'S NOT ASSISTING THE MILITARY IN KEEPING THE PEACE WORLDWIDE, BILLIONAIRE INDUSTRIALIST AND THIS YEAR'S MOST ELIGIBLE BACHELOR TONY STARK CAN BE SEEN ENJOYING THE NIGHTLIFE AT THE HOTTEST SPOTS ON FIVE CONTINENTS--
IRON MA
TVT NEWS

--JUST LAST NIGHT, THE PAPARAZZI WERE HOT ON HIS TRAIL IN MANHATTAN WHEN HE STUMBLED OUT OF THE GUGGENHEIM AFTER A GALA EVENT...
I HOPE HE KNOWS WHAT HE'S DOING, PEPPER.
EARLY NIGHT FOR ME, FOLKS. I NEED MY BEAUTY SLEEP.
CHECK OUT W.H.i.H. NEWS TOMORROW FOR THE FULL SCOOP.
DOESN'T CHERYL STILL LIVE ON CENTRAL PARK WEST...?
SHARON, SIR.
RIGHT. OKAY, SHE'LL DO.
THAT REPULSOR TECH IN HIS CHEST IS CAUSING A BIT OF INTERFERENCE.
ADJUST THE FREQUENCY. YOU CAN DIAL IT IN...
...AND IT'S MIDNIGHT. TIME TO CHECK IN.
I'M ON IT.
EAGLE EYES TO EAGLE'S NEST. SCRAMBLE CODE EPSILON.
TRANSMITTING...
...HE'S LEAVING THE FUNDRAISER NOW, SIR. HEADING TO A PERSONAL RESIDENCE ON CENTRAL PARK WEST WITH HIS DRIVER.
WE'RE GOING MOBILE NOW.
KEEP ON IT, EAGLE EYES.
DON'T LET HIM OUT OF YOUR SIGHT.

MISTER STARK HAS GIVEN ME FULL AUTHORITY TO MAKE SURE THAT THE V.A. HOSPITAL FUND IS FRONT AND CENTER IN THE NEWS PIECES YOU'LL SEE TONIGHT.
DOES ANYBODY HAVE A FINAL TALLY ON THE BOX OFFICE TOTALS--
DEET DEET
EXCUSE ME. I NEED TO TAKE THIS...
DO YOU MIND? I'M DOING WHAT I CAN TO MAKE YOU LOOK LESS LIKE A GLORY HOUND.
GLORY HOUND? THIS IS FOR CHARITY, POTTS--!
BESIDES, ONE OF 'EM IS HAVING A BIT OF ENGINE TROUBLE. CHECK IT OUT...
U.S. NAVY
U.S. NAVY

DON'T TRY TO KID A KIDDER, COLONEL. I *SAW* THE WAY YOU WERE EYEBALLING THE SUIT.

LIKE A KID ON CHRISTMAS EVE.

CAN YOU *BLAME* ME? FOR A PILOT, THAT SUIT IS THE *ULTIMATE.*

WHAT I WOULDN'T *GIVE* FOR A TURN IN THERE...

COLONEL, I APPRECIATE THE SENTIMENT...

...BUT THIS ISN'T THE LATEST MODEL HORNET OFF THE BOEING ASSEMBLY LINE, IS IT?

HAVING SAID THAT, YOU AND THE BLUES DO GREAT WORK AND I'M GLAD I WAS HERE TO HELP OUT.

POTTS.

YOU WORK FOR ME. THE SILENT TREATMENT? NOT QUITE CONDUCIVE TO THE EMPLOYER-EMPLOYEE DYNAMIC.

YOU LOOK GREAT IN THAT OUTFIT, BY THE WAY.

LIEUTENANT COLONEL RHODES WANTS TO SPEAK TO YOU.

I TOLD HIM TO MEET YOU AT THE HOUSE.

"LIEUTENANT COLONEL RHODES"?

WHY DON'T YOU JUST CALL HIM *RHODEY* LIKE THE REST OF US?

YOU HAVE A VISITOR, SIR...
YEAH, I GOT THAT, J.A.R.V.I.S.
TO WHAT DO I OWE THE PLEASURE...?
I THINK YOU KNOW.
SINCE YOU MADE YOUR LITTLE ANNOUNCEMENT, I'VE DISCOVERED A NEW HOBBY...
...COVERING YOUR ASS.
SO, WHAT YOU'RE SAYING IS...YOU'RE HERE ON BUSINESS UNRELATED TO YOUR GIG AS MILITARY LIAISON TO MY COMPANY.
JUST WANTED TO BE SURE.
C'MON DOWNSTAIRS...
LOOK, I KNOW YOU'VE BEEN RUNNING INTERFERENCE FOR ME WHEN I'VE GONE OFF THE RESERVATION.
WELCOME BACK, SIR. I'VE GOT DIAGNOSTIC ANALYSIS ON THE NEW MODEL UNITS...
UPLOAD IT TO THE SIMULATOR, J.A.R.V.I.S.
JUST ANSWER ME THIS...WAS THAT YOU THAT HIT THAT DEPOT IN PAVLODAR...?

YOU THINK I'VE GOT ANY INTEREST IN A TEN RINGS SECT IN CAHOOTS WITH ROGUE RUSSIAN NATIONALISTS? C'MON...!
BUT I WILL SAY THIS: AS A VACATION SPOT, YOU COULD DO WORSE THAN KAZAKHSTAN IN THE SPRING.
YO! ON THE FLIPSIDE!
BUT YOU'VE CONFIRMED THE TEN RINGS WERE INVOLVED. FINE.
OKAY, WELL...AT LEAST THE HOSTAGES ARE OKAY. COULD'VE GOTTEN PRETTY MESSY HAD THINGS GONE A DIFFERENT WAY.
INNOCENT PEOPLE COULD'VE DIED.
NOT ON MY WATCH.
C'MON, MAN...IT'S A MATTER OF PROTOCOL.
I'M JUST TRYING TO TELL YOU...YOU'RE MAKING PEOPLE NERVOUS. HALF THE TIME, YOU'RE RUSHING IN AND DEALING WITH SITUATIONS BEFORE WE CAN OFFICIALLY DEPLOY YOU.
PROTOCOL?! CAN I HELP IT IF YOU GUYS MOVE TOO SLOW...?
THAT'S NOT THE POINT.
THEN WHAT IS THE POINT?
THE POINT IS... WE'RE SUPPOSED TO BE WORKING TOGETHER.

APPRECIATE THAT. I REALLY DO.
YOU TRY LIVING WITH ARC REACTOR TECH SITTING IN YOUR CHEST.
IF IT WASN'T FOR THIS, THERE WOULDN'T BE AN IRON MAN.
I KNOW.
THEY'VE GOT ME WRITING A REPORT ON YOU NOW...
REALLY? WELL, BE SURE TO SEND A COPY OVER. I'LL GIVE IT A GLANCE.
OR YOU COULD JUST TELL ME WHAT IT SAYS. YOU GONNA THROW ME UNDER THE BUS OR WHAT?
I CAN TAKE IT.
PLEASE. I'M GOING TO ASSESS THE SITUATION AND OFFER MY RECOMMENDATION.
I'M STILL THE BEST ALLY YOU'RE GOING TO HAVE...
...REMEMBER THAT.
RHODEY--

PRIORITY ALERT COMING THROUGH NOW. GRABBED OFF THE SATELLITE FEEDS...
PATCH ME IN, J.A.R.V.I.S.
TONY, THIS IS EXACTLY WHAT I'M TALKING ABOUT--
BZZT BZZT BZZT
RHODES.
...
YES, SIR.
...
YES, SIR. I AM.
ACTUALLY, I THINK HE'S GOT THE INTEL ALREADY, SIR.
...
I'LL TELL HIM.
YES, SIR.
TONY--!
THEY WANT YOU TO DO SOME RECONNAISSANCE FIRST. WHATEVER'S BEING REPORTED ON IN AL KUT IS--
PEOPLE ARE DYING, RHODEY...
...THAT MEANS FULL SPEED AHEAD.

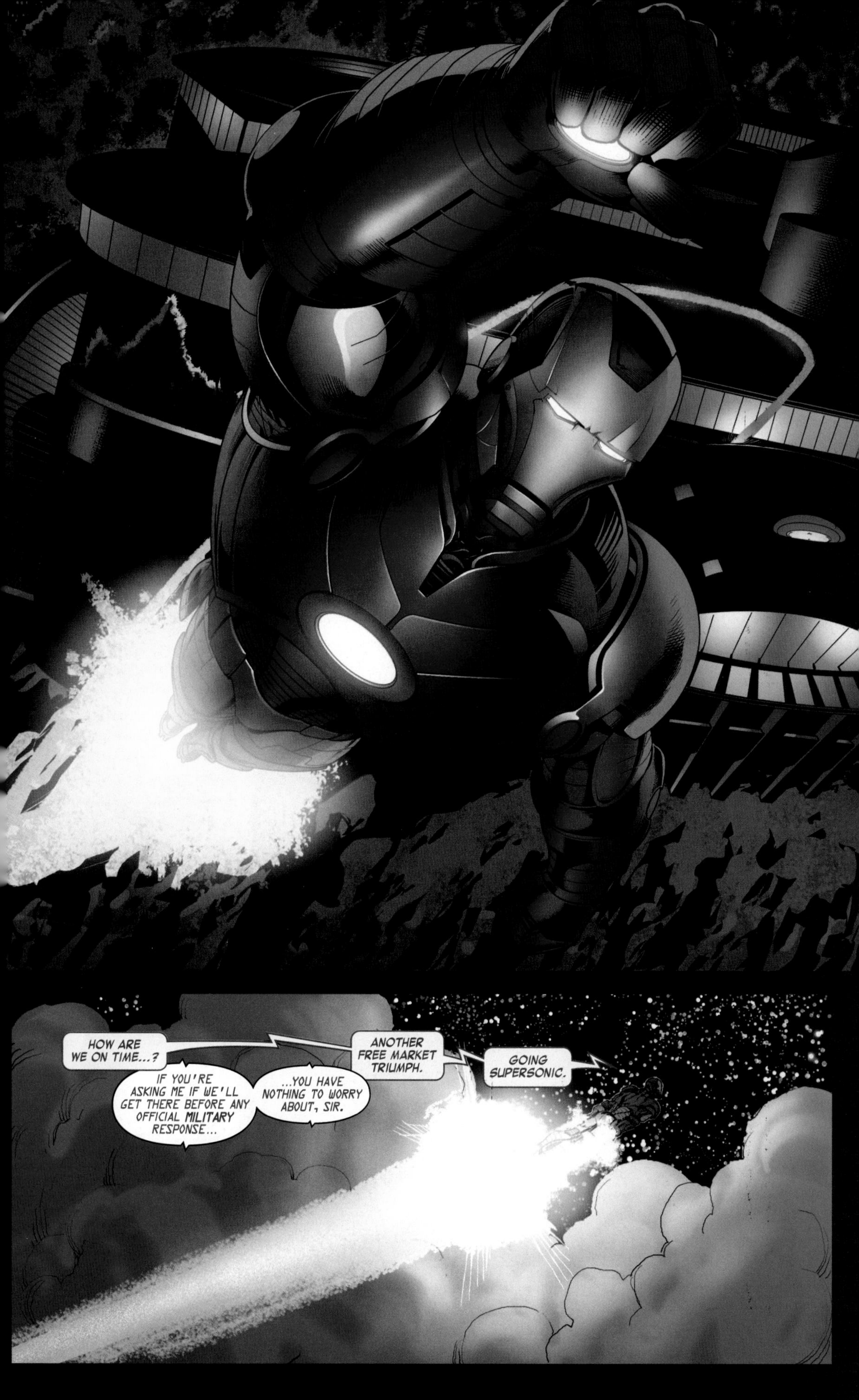
HOW ARE WE ON TIME...?
IF YOU'RE ASKING ME IF WE'LL GET THERE BEFORE ANY OFFICIAL MILITARY RESPONSE...
...YOU HAVE NOTHING TO WORRY ABOUT, SIR.
ANOTHER FREE MARKET TRIUMPH.
GOING SUPERSONIC.

UN

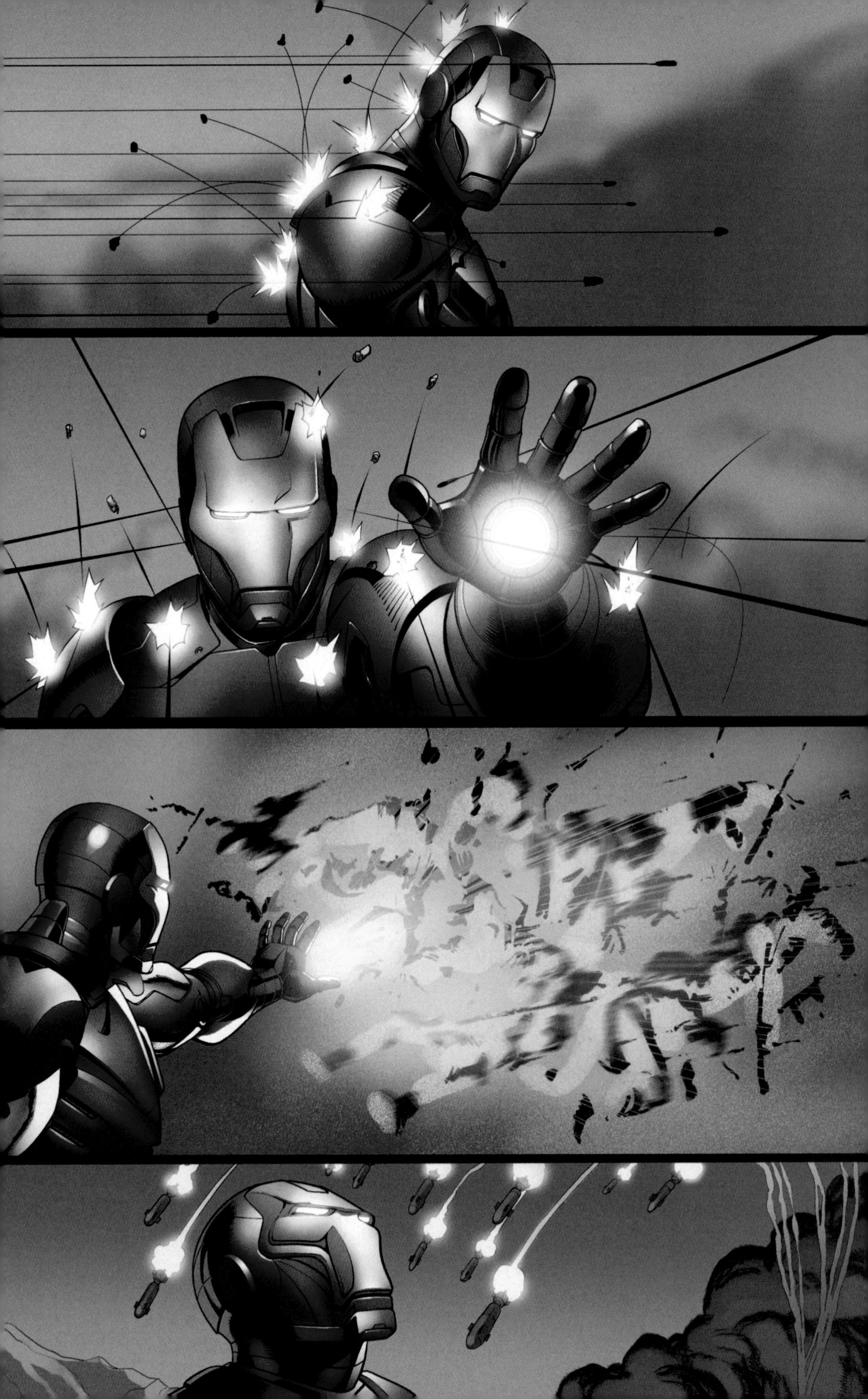

RIGHT.

NEGATIVE VITALS ON ENEMY TARGETS.
YEAH, I FIGURED.
WHERE'S THE NEWS CREW...?

STARK!
OVER HERE!

YOU GUYS GOOD OVER HERE?
MY PRODUCER GOT TAGGED IN THE SHOULDER. HE'LL BE ALL RIGHT.
AT LEAST THE RED CROSS CAN GET IN NOW. THEY'VE BEEN KEEPING THEIR DISTANCE DURING THESE INSURGENT ATTACKS.
WELL, I GUESS I OWE YOU. YOU MAKE MY JOB A LOT EASIER.
HOW DO YOU THINK I FOUND OUT WHAT WAS HAPPENING HERE IN THE FIRST PLACE?
ARE YOU KIDDING? WE WERE COUNTING ON IT.
WE KNOW YOUR M.O. BY NOW.
FAIR ENOUGH.
SO, YOU GOT ALL THAT?
ARE YOU USING THE STRK-HD?
HELL, YEAH.
OF COURSE.
GOOD. I GOT THE ALL-CLEAR FROM YOUR BOSSES IN ATLANTA TO DOWNLOAD THE FOOTAGE STRAIGHT TO MY P.R. DEPARTMENT.
HEY, DO ME A FAVOR...IN THE WRAP-UP, DON'T REFER TO ME AS "STARK."
TRYIN' TO BUILD A BRAND HERE.
OKAY, FELLAS...I'M OUTTA HERE BEFORE THE CAVALRY ARRIVES. I DON'T LIKE TO DEBRIEF ONSITE.

...IRON MAN'S ARRIVAL SIGNALED NOT ONLY A DRASTIC ESCALATION IN COMBAT, BUT ALSO A SWIFT RESOLUTION TO THE INSURGENT ATTACK ON THE AIR BASE HERE THAT LED TO THE DEATHS OF SEVERAL U.N. PEACEKEEPING TROOPS.
SO FAR, U.S. MILITARY OFFICIALS HAVE NO COMMENT ON WHAT ARE CLEARLY UNSANCTIONED ACTIONS ON HIS PART.
UNSANCTIONED OR NOT, AS FAR AS THIS REPORTER IS CONCERNED...THOSE ACTIONS ARE MOST WELCOME.
WHiH
WORLD NEWS
A W.H.i.H. NOBODY THINKS HE'S WALTER CRONKITE.
IT'S GETTING WORSE, LIEUTENANT COLONEL.
HE'S A FRIEND, SENATOR. A GOOD FRIEND. AND I TALKED TO HIM.
WELL, HE'S NOT LISTENING.
THIS IS A MATTER OF NATIONAL SECURITY AND HE'S NOT LISTENING.
WHAT DID HE SAY?
HE'S PRETTY ADAMANT. I DON'T KNOW IF HE'S EVER GOING TO COMPLETELY FALL IN LINE. HE'S GOT HIS OWN IDEAS ON HOW THINGS SHOULD HAPPEN.
PERSONALLY, I CAN SEE THE MERIT IN HIS--
WELL, I'M SICK OF WAITING.
I'VE ASKED SOMEONE HERE WHO MIGHT BE ABLE TO TACKLE THIS PROBLEM FROM A DIFFERENT ANGLE. I'M SURE YOU'VE HEARD OF HIM...
...GENERAL THADDEUS ROSS.

GENERAL.
AT EASE, SON.
GENTLEMEN, YOU'LL FORGIVE ME, I'M IN A BIT OF A HURRY. THIS IS TAKING ME AWAY FROM THE GAMMA PROJECT AND I'D LIKE TO GET BACK TO IT.
SENATOR STERN, I'M ASSUMING YOU'VE BRIEFED HIM?
THE SET-UP, YES. I WAS WAITING FOR YOU TO PROVIDE THE PUNCHLINE.
NOTHING FUNNY ABOUT THIS, SENATOR. YOU PEOPLE WANT ME ACTING AS "SUPERHUMAN WATCHDOG," AND TONY STARK IS A PRIME EXAMPLE.
THE U.S. ARMY CAN'T AFFORD TO WAIT FOR HIM TO SMARTEN UP.
COME WITH ME.
OBVIOUSLY, WHAT YOU'RE ABOUT TO SEE HAS BEEN CLASSIFIED TOP SECRET...
WHERE'S HAMMER?
HE'S ON HIS WAY. HIS DESIGN SPECS PLUS OUR OWN ARMY ENGINEERS CAME UP WITH SOMETHING DEFINITIVE IN THE AREA OF STRATEGIC MOBILE WEAPONRY.
THIS WILL UNDOUBTEDLY SEND THE RIGHT MESSAGE TO THE ENEMIES OF FREEDOM.
WHICH IS...
...WE DON'T NEED TONY STARK.
OH, NO.

GOD BLESS AMERICA.

IRON MAN: PUBLIC IDENTITY #2
COVER BY ADI GRANOV

THE GULF OF ADEN:
CROSS-CHECKING WITH THE INTERNATIONAL MARITIME BUREAU, SIR. AWAITING CONFIRMATION FROM ECOTERRA.
NOT NECESSARY, J.A.R.V.I.S.
I KNOW SOMALI PIRATES WHEN I SEE THEM...
...AND I KNOW EXACTLY HOW TO DEAL WITH THEM.

DECADES AGO:
ANTON...
...WHAT HAVE YOU DONE?
WHAT ANY MAN WOULD DO IN MY POSITION.
DON'T ACT SO SHOCKED, HOWARD. YOU SHOULD KNOW BETTER THAN ANYONE...
...IT'S ALL ABOUT MONEY.

WE'VE ALREADY ROUNDED UP VANKO'S FAMILY IN TOWN.
DON'T WORRY, MISTER STARK. WE'LL TAKE CARE OF THINGS FROM HERE.
I KNOW THAT MUST'VE BEEN TOUGH, HOWARD...
...BUT THE GUY WAS A CROOK. WHAT CHOICE DID YOU HAVE?
YOU TOOK THAT COMMIE UNDER YOUR WING. YOU LET HIM INTO YOUR HOME.
OBADIAH...
I KNOW THIS CUTS CLOSER TO THE BONE BECAUSE OF YOUR BELIEF IN THE ARC REACTOR...YOUR PLANS FOR THE EXPO...
I'M JUST SAYING...MAYBE YOU SHOULD TAKE THIS INCIDENT AS SOME SORT OF SIGN.

HEY.
I'M HERE FOR YOU. JUST LIKE I'VE ALWAYS BEEN.
BUT LET'S JUST GET BACK TO DOING WHAT WE DO BEST, HUH?
YEARS LATER:
DAMMIT--!
TONY--!
WHERE THE HELL ARE YOU?!
DAD...?

THIS IS *YOURS*, I TAKE IT?!
IS *THIS* HOW YOU SPEND YOUR WEEKEND AT HOME?!
D-DAD, I--
WASTE OF TIME!
I DON'T *NEED* TO DEAL WITH THIS *NONSENSE!*
DO YOU UNDERSTAND ME--?!
I WANNA GO BACK TO SCHOOL...
I WANNA GO BACK TO SCHOOL...
I WANNA GO BACK TO SCHOOL...
MASTER TONY.
DO NOT TAKE HIS OUTBURST TO HEART.
LEAVE ME ALONE, JARVIS.
FATHERS AND SONS. THAT PARTICULAR RELATIONSHIP...

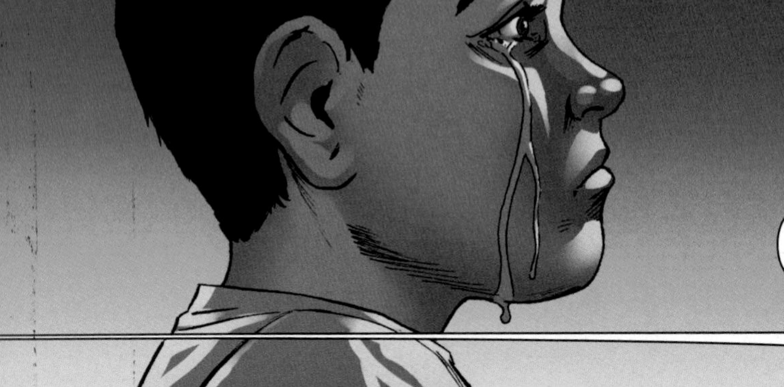

"TIME HEALS ALL WOUNDS..."
PARDON ME, SIR...
...DID YOU SAY SOMETHING?
NOT REALLY. JUST REMEMBERING A HALLMARK CARD SOMEONE SENT ME ONCE.
PROBABLY THE SAME ONE THAT SAID "YOU CAN'T GO HOME AGAIN."
BUT THIS ISN'T REALLY HOME, IS IT...?
THEN FOR WHAT PURPOSE DID YOU INSTALL ME HERE?
FORCE OF HABIT, J.A.R.V.I.S.-- YOU'VE ALWAYS BEEN HERE...

...EVERY TIME I'D VISIT FROM BOARDING SCHOOL, YOU WERE THE HAPPIEST TO SEE ME.
I DON'T RECALL, SIR.
OKAY, NEVER MIND.
HE NEVER LET ME COME IN HERE. I HAD TO SNEAK IN WHEN HE WAS OUT OF THE HOUSE.
FIGURES I NEVER FOUND ANYTHING GOOD...
SIR, I HATE TO DISPEL YOUR DARK CLOUDS OF NOSTALGIA, BUT WE HAVE A PRIORITY ALERT COMING THROUGH.
DIVERTING TO YOUR HANDHELD...
UNCLE SAM CALLING...?
NOW THERE'S SOMEONE WHO'S GOT A FUNNY WAY OF SHOWING HOW MUCH HE LOVES ME...
HMMM.
OH, THIS I CANNOT STAND...
...TIME FOR ANOTHER DESERT VACATION.

AHHH...SMELL THAT NIGHT AIR, HUH? THAT'S BRACING...!
ARE YOU RHODES...?
LIEUTENANT COLONEL RHODES.
FAIR ENOUGH.
JUSTIN HAMMER. GOOD TO SEE YOU.
LISTEN, I KNOW YOU'RE PALS WITH STARK. THICK AS THIEVES AND WHATNOT. DON'T WORRY, I'M NOT GONNA HOLD THAT AGAINST YOU...
...BESIDES, I CAN'T HELP IT IF STARK WON'T PLAY BALL WITH THE MILITARY AND I WILL.
SPEAKING OF WHICH...
...HELLO, GENIUS.

BEAUTIFUL, ISN'T IT...?
AN AERODYNAMIC MARVEL. THE NEXT STEP IN CLOSE-QUARTER COMBAT. FULL PROTECTION AND ATTACK CAPABILITIES.
YOU OKAY IN THERE, AIRMAN...?

NEVER BETTER, SIR.
SHE HANDLES LIKE A *DREAM*. WHOEVER *DESIGNED* HER--
HELLO. HI. YOU'RE *LOOKING* AT HIM.
AND YOU'RE *WELCOME*.

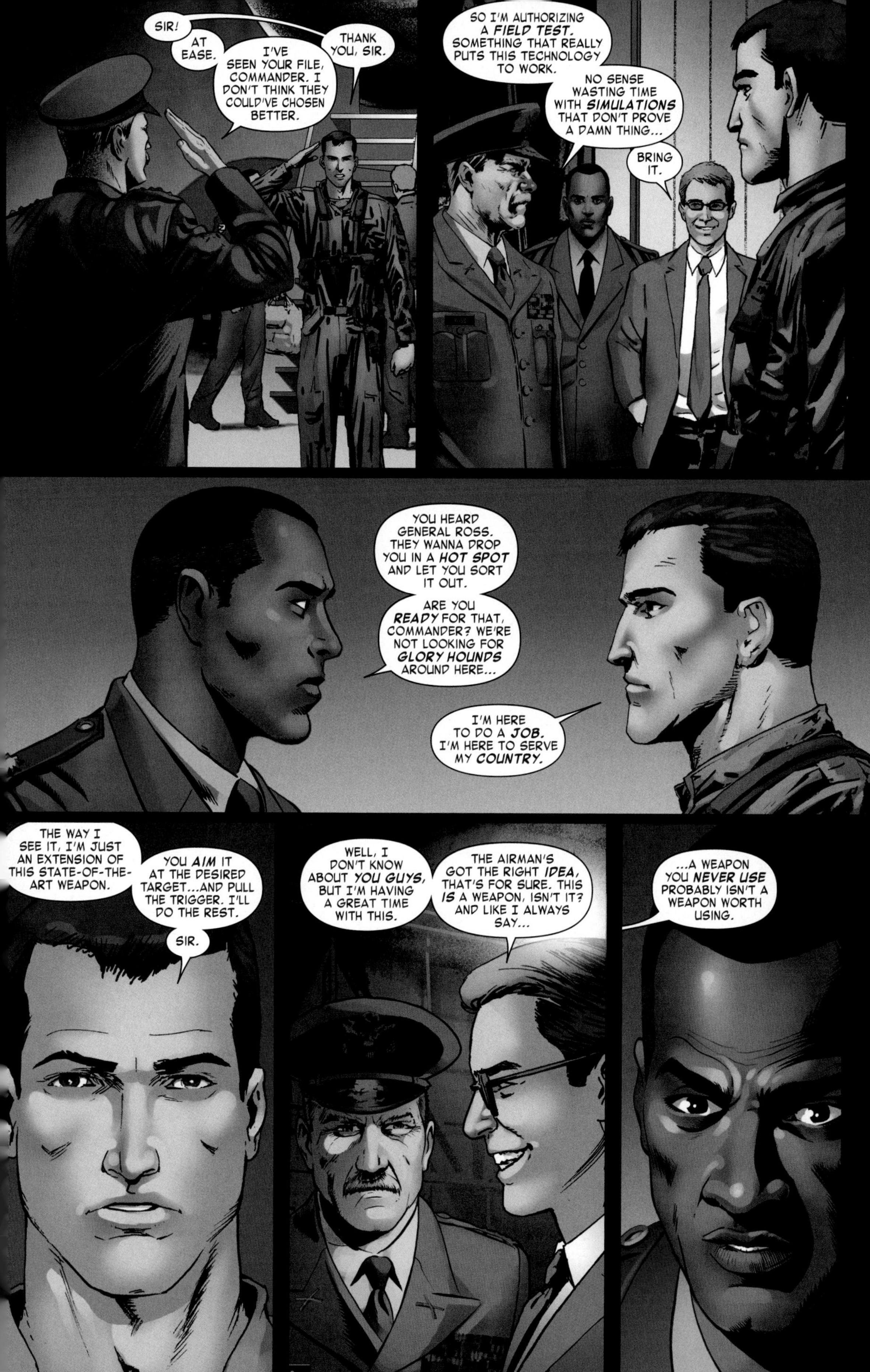
SIR!
AT EASE.
I'VE SEEN YOUR FILE, COMMANDER. I DON'T THINK THEY COULD'VE CHOSEN BETTER.
THANK YOU, SIR.
SO I'M AUTHORIZING A FIELD TEST. SOMETHING THAT REALLY PUTS THIS TECHNOLOGY TO WORK.
NO SENSE WASTING TIME WITH SIMULATIONS THAT DON'T PROVE A DAMN THING...
BRING IT.
YOU HEARD GENERAL ROSS. THEY WANNA DROP YOU IN A HOT SPOT AND LET YOU SORT IT OUT.
ARE YOU READY FOR THAT, COMMANDER? WE'RE NOT LOOKING FOR GLORY HOUNDS AROUND HERE...
I'M HERE TO DO A JOB. I'M HERE TO SERVE MY COUNTRY.
THE WAY I SEE IT, I'M JUST AN EXTENSION OF THIS STATE-OF-THE-ART WEAPON.
YOU AIM IT AT THE DESIRED TARGET...AND PULL THE TRIGGER. I'LL DO THE REST.
SIR.
WELL, I DON'T KNOW ABOUT YOU GUYS, BUT I'M HAVING A GREAT TIME WITH THIS.
THE AIRMAN'S GOT THE RIGHT IDEA, THAT'S FOR SURE. THIS IS A WEAPON, ISN'T IT? AND LIKE I ALWAYS SAY...
...A WEAPON YOU NEVER USE PROBABLY ISN'T A WEAPON WORTH USING.

"I CAN ASSURE ALL OF YOU..."
STARK
STARK
...MISTER STARK IS MOST DEFINITELY ON HIS WAY.
I KNOW THIS ISN'T THE FIRST TIME HE'S MISSED A BOARD MEETING, BUT YOU UNDERSTAND THAT THE NATURE OF HIS SCHEDULE MEANS THAT SOMETIMES--
DEET DEET DEET
EXCUSE ME, EVERYBODY...
...SPEAK OF THE DEVIL.
DO YOU KNOW WHERE I AM RIGHT NOW...?!
UMMM... KEEPING MY SEAT WARM AT THE BOARD MEETING? FORCING A SMILE LIKE EVERYTHING'S FINE?
I'M TRYING TO MAINTAIN THE ILLUSION OF YOUR SANITY.
SO FAR, SO GOOD, BUT YOU NEED TO--
NO CAN DO, POTTS. I'M NOT EXACTLY IN THE NEIGHBORHOOD...

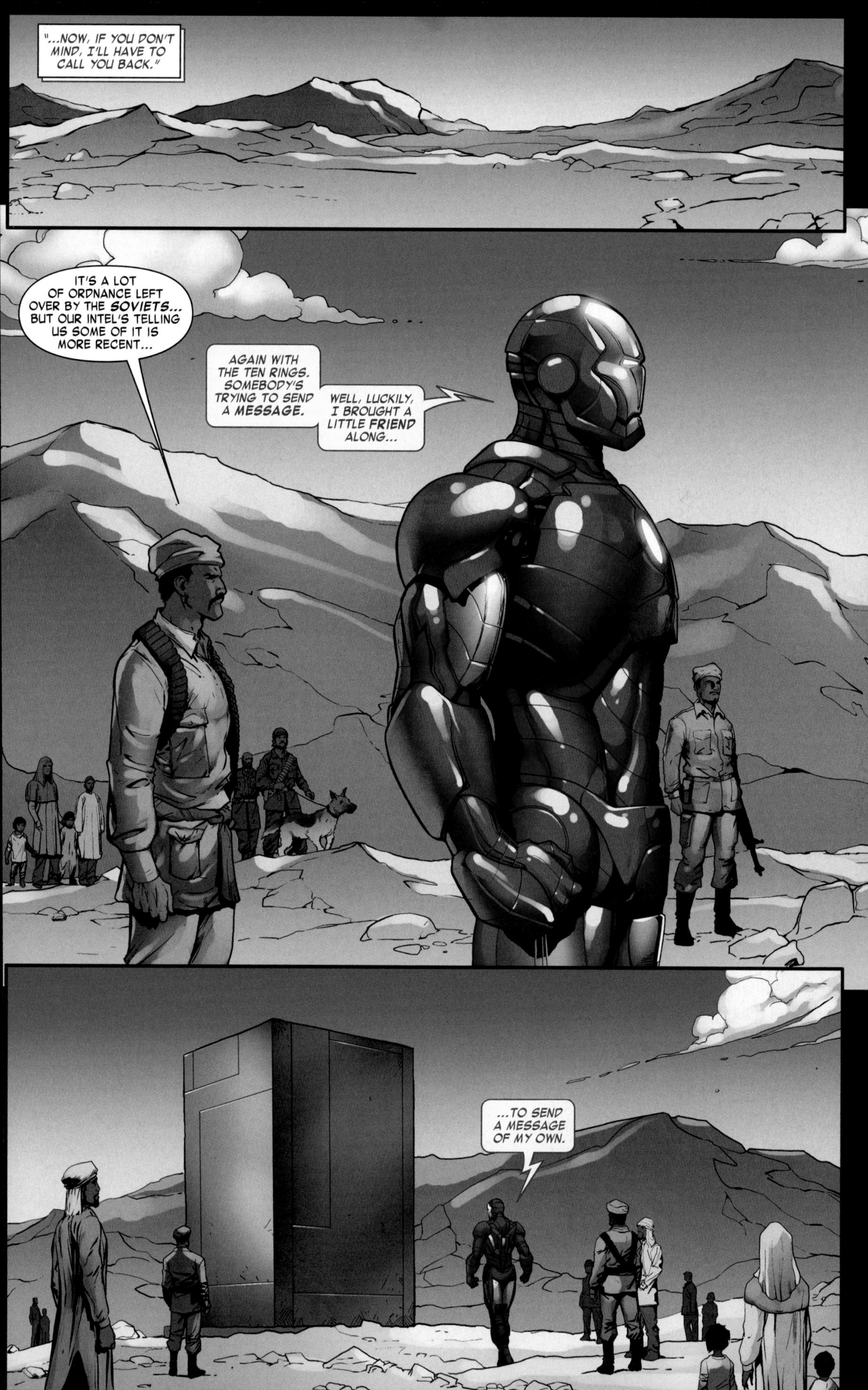
"...NOW, IF YOU DON'T MIND, I'LL HAVE TO CALL YOU BACK."
IT'S A LOT OF ORDNANCE LEFT OVER BY THE SOVIETS... BUT OUR INTEL'S TELLING US SOME OF IT IS MORE RECENT...
AGAIN WITH THE TEN RINGS. SOMEBODY'S TRYING TO SEND A MESSAGE.
WELL, LUCKILY, I BROUGHT A LITTLE FRIEND ALONG...
...TO SEND A MESSAGE OF MY OWN.

NEVER LET IT BE SAID THAT I SHOW UP TO A PARTY EMPTY-HANDED.
THIS JUST HAPPENS TO BE SOMETHING I'VE BEEN WORKING ON IN WHAT LITTLE SPARE TIME I HAVE...
FEAST YOUR EYES ON THE MAGNA-DRONE.
PATENT PENDING.
THIS'LL ONLY TAKE A FEW MINUTES, FOLKS.
J.A.R.V.I.S., YOU KNOW WHAT TO DO...
ALL DRONE SYSTEMS ARE READY. AWAITING YOUR ORDER, SIR...
LAUNCH.

I'VE GOT TELEMETRY. AUXILIARY BOOST ON MY MARK. LET'S KEEP IT AT A SAFE ALTITUDE, JUST IN CASE.
READY TO INITIATE...
"...LET'S OPEN HER UP."

NOW THAT'S WHAT I'M TALKING ABOUT.
WE'RE READING A 100% RETRIEVAL RATE AS WELL AS NON-DETONATION...
WELL, IT'S PRETTY OBVIOUS FROM HERE THAT IT'S A RAGING SUCCESS...
...CHALK UP ANOTHER ONE FOR GOOD OL' AMERICAN INGENUITY.
HOW 'BOUT WE POP UP TO TOKYO TO CELEBRATE?

WELL, IT CERTAINLY WORKED.
SEVERAL SQUARE MILES OF AFGHANI DESERT... COMPLETELY CLEAN. PRETTY IMPRESSIVE, COLONEL FURY.
YEAH, HE'S QUITE THE HUMANITARIAN...
...FIGHTING THE GOOD FIGHT IN THE ALTRUISTIC NAME OF WORLD PEACE.
LET'S JUST KEEP WATCHING. SEE WHAT HE DOES NEXT.
SOMETHING IN MY GUT TELLS ME THIS WON'T LAST FOREVER.
HE'S STILL FLYING BLIND.

...WE'LL TAKE HER DOWN BELOW RADAR IN TWO MINUTES.
FANTASTIC.
YOU KNOW, I LIKE YOU, GENERAL. SO MUCH, IN FACT, THAT I'M GONNA CUT YOU GUYS A DEAL WHEN YOU WANT TO BUY A *FLEET* OF THESE...
HAT MATTERS OW...IS THAT I ET *RESULTS.*
COCKPIT! LET'S LIGHT THIS CANDLE.
RIGHT. WE'RE OVER THE TARGET AREA.
OPENING BOMB BAY DOORS...
...PREPARE FOR PERSONNEL DROP.
ONBOARD SYSTEMS ONLINE. FINAL DIAGNOSTICS COMPLETE.
I AM OKAY TO GO.

HE'S CLEAR.
OF COURSE HE IS.
THRUSTERS IGNITE.
GOING RADIO SILENT.

WHEW!
TAKE YOUR TIME, FELLAS.
IT'S NOT LIKE I HAVEN'T BEEN INSIDE THIS CAN FOR NINETEEN HOURS PLUS OR ANYTHING LIKE THAT.
WELCOME BACK...
...DID YOU HAVE A NICE HOLIDAY?
GOOD ONE, POTTS. DID YOU TRY THESE JOKES OUT ON THE BOARD FIRST?
GOD, I NEED A SHOWER.
YOU...RUN A THERMAL IMAGING PROGRAM ON THE RIGHT ARM GAUNTLET WHILE I'M GONE. FULL CIRCUIT SCAN.
TONY, I'M GOING TO TELL YOU WHAT I CAN. AS A FRIEND, I FEEL LIKE I HAVE TO. HOWEVER, KEEP IN MIND THAT I CAN'T COMPROMISE ANY CLASSIFIED INFO.
JUSTIN HAMMER'S GOTTEN FRIENDLY WITH MY SUPERIORS.
VERY FRIENDLY.
AND YOU'VE BEEN COMING ACROSS AS MORE AND MORE... INDEPENDENT WHEN IT COMES TO THE WORK YOU'RE DOING FOR THEM.

THE "WORK"? LISTEN, I WAS CALLED IN TO DO A LITTLE GARDENING OUTSIDE OF KABUL. I'M SURE YOU'VE READ THE BRIEF BY NOW, RHODEY.
CAN HAMMER'S NEW TOY--WHATEVER IT IS--DO THAT?
THAT'S NOT THE POINT AND YOU KNOW IT.
THEY WANT IT TO DO WHAT YOU WON'T DO. THEY WANT A WEAPON.
WELL, THEY'RE RIGHT. I'M NOT THEIR WEAPON...
...THAT'S NOT WHY I WENT TO KABUL. YOU KNOW WHY I WENT? THE REAL REASON?
DOGS.
MINE-DETECTING DOGS. GERMAN SHEPHERDS BEING TRAINED ALONG WITH THEIR AFGHANI HANDLERS TO SNIFF OUT THESE LANDMINES.
THEY WERE GREAT AT FINDING SOME OF THE OLD SOVIET STUFF. BUT THE TEN RINGS HAVE BEEN USING THOSE OLD MINEFIELDS TO PLACE THEIR OWN EXPLOSIVES THAT WERE KILLING THESE POOR CANINES.
YOU WENT OVER THERE...
...TO SAVE THE DOGS...?
HEY. POTTS.
I KNOW YOU'RE WORRIED. BUT DON'T BE. I KNOW WHAT I'M DOING.

MORE IMPORTANTLY, I KNOW WHY I'M DOING IT. I DON'T HAVE A CHOICE ANYMORE.
SO LET'S BOTH MOVE ON TO SOMETHING MORE IMPORTANT, LIKE MAYBE--
BZZT BZZT BZZT
THAT'S ME.
WELL, I KNEW IT WASN'T ME.
HOLD ON. I HAVE TO TAKE THIS.
SUCH A PROFESSIONAL.
RHODES.
...
WAIT... SAY THAT AGAIN?!
WHAT HAPPENED--?!
FOR GOD'S SAKE--! OPEN UP THE SAT FEEDS NOW!
SHUT UP! I WANT TO KNOW WHERE HE IS--
IT WASN'T SUPPOSED TO BE VULNERABLE TO ANY KIND OF SURFACE-TO-AIR--

NO, NO, NO--!
THE CONGOLESE ARMY'S ALREADY ON TOP OF HIM?!
SO THIS IS CONFIRMED--
--YOU'RE TELLING ME WE'VE GOT A MAN DOWN IN UNFRIENDLY TERRITORY...!
TONY--
WHAT CHOICE DO I HAVE, POTTS?
DAMMIT.

IRON MAN: PUBLIC IDENTITY #2
COVER BY ADI GRANOV

SEN. STERN'S OFFICE:
ARE YOU SERIOUS?!
WELL, I'VE GOT HAMMER'S PR PIECE ON MY DVD RIGHT NOW...! AND YOU'RE TELLING ME--
...NATIONAL SECURITY IS OUR HIGHEST PRIORITY... AND THIS IS THE GAME-CHANGER! FROM THE BRILLIANT MIND OF WEAPONS DESIGNER AND WIRED'S MOST ELIGIBLE TECH-BACHELOR, JUSTIN HAMMER...
AND WE'RE NOT EVEN SUPPOSED TO BE IN THAT REGION...!
OH MY GOD.
GET ME GENERAL ROSS--
...THIS STATE-OF-THE-ART, SINGLE PILOT ATTACK CRAFT IS THE NEXT STEP IN WARFARE TECHNOLOGY. AND OUT OF THOUSANDS OF CANDIDATES, THIS BRAVE AIRMAN HAS BEEN CHOSEN TO FLY IT. HIS MISSION IS CLEAR...
I AM AMERICA'S DUTIFUL SERVANT.

DECADES AGO:
TONY--!
I HAVEN'T BEEN BACK FROM CAMBRIDGE TWELVE HOURS...
...CAN'T THIS WAIT?
LISTEN, KID, I'M THE ONE PERSON WHO'S NOT GOING TO AUTOMATICALLY FALL TO THEIR KNEES WHEN SOMEONE SAYS, "SUMMA CUM LAUDE."
TWELVE HOURS IS A LIFETIME.
YOU PLOWED THROUGH SCHOOL FOR A REASON. AND DON'T TELL ME IT WAS JUST BECAUSE YOU WERE BORED.
NOW DON'T TELL ME YOU'RE JUST GOING TO--
DEEP BREATH, DAD. I CAN'T CONQUER THE WORLD UNTIL I WORK ON MY TAN.
SIGH
TONY, I KNOW WE HAVEN'T EXACTLY SEEN EYE-TO-EYE WHEN IT COMES TO--
AHEM! SIR...

...MRS. STARK IS WAITING FOR YOU IN THE CAR.
OKAY, JARVIS. THANK YOU.
TELL HER I'LL BE RIGHT OUT.
HEAR THAT? DON'T KEEP MOM WAITING. WE BOTH KNOW HOW WOMEN ARE...
WE CAN PLAN THE REST OF MY LIFE WHEN YOU GET BACK. I PROMISE I'LL STAY OUT OF THE LIQUOR CABINET WHILE YOU'RE GONE.
TONY...
...THE LEVEL OF YOUR INTELLIGENCE DOESN'T ALWAYS CORRESPOND TO THE LEVEL OF YOUR MATURITY. I THINK YOU KNOW THAT.
THERE'S A LOT ABOUT WHAT I DO THAT I HAVEN'T TOLD YOU. THINGS I WANT YOU TO KNOW. THINGS YOU NEED TO KNOW.
I JUST HOPE...THIS PHASE YOU'RE IN DOESN'T LAST FOREVER.
"THIS PHASE..."
I KNOW WHAT I'M DOING, OLD MAN...

"THIS WAS NOT PART OF THE PLAN..."

...SOMEONE AUTHORIZED THIS PARTICULAR "FIELD TEST"?!
I SEE. YES, SIR.

HERE IT COMES...
I THINK YOU CAN GUESS WHERE THIS IS GOING...

...HAMMER'S PROTOTYPE. THEY PUT IT INTO ACTION. I KNEW THEY WOULD, BUT I'LL BE DAMNED IF THEY DIDN'T SEND IT INTO NORTH KIVU PROVINCE.
AN AIRMAN WAS TRAINED TO PILOT IT...
Call Ended 3:24

...NOW HE'S BEING HELD CAPTIVE.

THIS IS EXACTLY WHAT I'VE BEEN TRYING TO TELL YOU. THESE PEOPLE HAVE BECOME IMPATIENT.
NOW WE'VE GOT ONE OF OUR OWN IN GRAVE DANGER. YOU HAVE TO--
I DON'T NEED A LECTURE, RHODEY--
DEET DEET DEET

SIR. AN INCOMING CALL FROM GENERAL TURNER AT THE PENTAGON.
RIGHT.
PUT IT ON SPEAKER, J.A.R.V.I.S....
GENERAL.
MISTER STARK, WE'VE GOT A BIT OF A PROBLEM WE'D LIKE YOU TO ADDRESS AS QUICKLY AS POSSIBLE.
APPARENTLY, WE'VE GOT SOME PROPRIETARY SURVEILLANCE TECHNOLOGY THAT'S GONE DOWN IN THE CONGO.
WE'VE GOT THE COORDINATES... BUT WITH THE ATROCITIES THAT ARE STILL BEING COMMITTED IN THAT REGION, WE THOUGHT--
GENERAL, YOU KNOW AS WELL AS I DO, THE CONGOLESE ARMY WON'T BE HAPPY TO SEE ME...
...NOT TO MENTION WHATEVER TERRORIST INFESTATION THAT'S OCCURRED IN THAT AREA.
SON, IF YOU ARE ENGAGED BY ENEMY FORCES, YOU HAVE EVERY RIGHT TO DEFEND YOURSELF--
I GET THE GIST, GENERAL. SEND ME THE COORDINATES.
TRANSMISSION ENDED, SIR.
I LOVE IT WHEN HE CALLS ME "SON"...
THEY JUST LIED TO YOU. THEY WANT YOU TO GO IN THERE AND--
HEY, POTTS...
...WORRY ABOUT GLOBAL WARMING. WORRY ABOUT HEALTH CARE IN AMERICA. WORRY ABOUT THE CALIFORNIA HOUSING MARKET.
THERE'S ALL SORTS OF GREAT THINGS TO WORRY ABOUT. BUT I'M NOT ONE OF THEM.
THIS IS WHAT I DO.
AND IT'S TIME TO GO TO WORK.

--TRYING TO PINPOINT HIS VITALS--
--HE'S STILL ON THE GRID!
...CAN'T EVEN SELF-DESTRUCT THE MECHANISM--!
--VIRTUAL UMBILICAL SYSTEMS INOPERATIVE!
KEEP THIS BIRD IN STEALTH MODE--!
SWITCHING OVER TO THERMAL IMAGING SWEEP...!
DAMMIT, I WANNA KNOW IF OUR MAN IS STILL ALIVE DOWN THERE!
SCRAMBLING COMM CODES!
I JUST WANNA SAY ONE THING ABOUT THOSE ANTI-AIRCRAFT AVOIDANCE SYSTEMS...
...THEY WERE FULLY RATED IN THE SIM CHAMBERS--
HAMMER--
--JUST SHUT THE HELL UP!
WE'RE NOT GONNA SCRUB THIS MISSION IF IT'S THE LAST THING--
GENERAL ROSS! RADAR'S GOT A BOGEY--
--MOVING IN FAST.
CROSS-REFERENCING SIGNAL...
...LOOKS LIKE THEY'RE SENDING IN IRON MAN TO CLEAN UP.
STARK...

"...MAYBE THIS WON'T
BE A WASH AFTER ALL."

JUST GOT WORD! WE CAN SCRAMBLE A TEAM OUT OF CAIRO AND GET THEM AIRBORNE WITHIN THE HOUR!
CONFIRMED! A SPECIAL FORCES UNIT--
WAIT!
WE'RE GOING TO HOLD BACK FOR A BIT...
...I WANT TO SEE EXACTLY WHAT THIS STARK CAN DO.
GUHHHT--!
KUHH--!

GHUHHT--!

<IT IS THE MAN OF IRON!*>
<TAKE HIM DOWN!>
*TRANSLATED FROM TSHILUBA
SO THEY WANT ME TO SLASH AND BURN THESE GUYS.
APPARENTLY, SIR.
WELL, I DON'T HAVE TIME FOR THAT...
SEISMIC IMAGING ONLINE...
...TARGETING.
NEED A LITTLE PERSONAL SPACE HERE, FELLAS--

SOMEONE PATCH ME IN SO I CAN TALK TO THIS SON OF A--
RIGHT AWAY, GENERAL.
WHAT THE HELL IS HE DOING DOWN THERE--?!
INCOMING MESSAGE. A-1 PRIORITY. FOUR-STAR.
LITTLE BUSY RIGHT NOW.
SIR...
FINE. PUT IT THROUGH.

YOU'VE GOT IRON MAN. WHO AM I TALKING TO...?
I'LL ASK THE QUESTIONS, STARK--
--THIS IS GENERAL THADDEUS ROSS! I'M IN COMMAND OF THIS OP AND WE'VE GOT A FIX ON YOUR POSITION!
YOU ARE ORDERED TO LAND AT CAIRO WEST AIR BASE IMMEDIATELY! AND YOU'D DAMN BETTER NOT TRY ANY--
GENERAL, YOU SOUND LIKE YOU'RE GOING TO HAVE A CORONARY...
...THAT'S NOT SOMETHING I WANT ON MY CONSCIENCE.
I'LL SEE YOU IN EGYPT.

THREE HOURS LATER:
THE WELCOME WAGON. NICE.
AFTER WHAT HE'S BEEN THROUGH...HE COULD USE A LITTLE HOSPITALITY.
CAREFUL. HE'S IN SHOCK.
GUYS, SPARE NO EXPENSE. ANYTHING THE AIR FORCE WON'T SPRING FOR, I WILL.
SO...GENERAL ROSS, I PRESUME.
YOU'VE GOT SOMETHING YOU WANT TO SAY TO ME...?
YOU BET YOUR TIN SUIT I DO--

--SATS PICKED UP A SHOOTOUT WITH THE CONGOLESE ARMY AND YOU DON'T RETURN FIRE?!
SOMEONE FIRES ON AN AMERICAN-- THAT AMERICAN FIRES BACK!
YEAH...I FIGURED THAT'S WHAT YOU GUYS WANTED ME TO DO.
THAT IS, IF HAMMER'S FOLLY COULDN'T DO THE JOB FOR YOU FIRST.
DON'T CONFUSE THE ISSUE, STARK! I KNOW YOU'VE BEEN DISTANCING YOURSELF FROM YOUR FATHER'S LEGACY--
--YOU CLAIM YOU'RE NO LONGER A WEAPONS MAKER-- BUT NOW YOU ARE THE WEAPON!
INTERESTING ANALYSIS OF MY LIFE'S WORK.
Y'KNOW, ON MY WAY HERE, I DECIDED TO RESEARCH YOU.
DID A LITTLE DIGGING. PULLED UP YOUR FILE...
THADDEUS ROSS
a.k.a. THUNDERBOLT
...QUITE A RESUME. YOU'VE HAD YOUR FINGERS IN A LOT OF PIES.
GENETIC ENHANCEMENTS FOR MILITARY EXPLOITATION. PRETTY ADVANCED FOR A SACRED COW LIKE YOU. NOT TO MENTION DICEY.
AND "THUNDERBOLT"...KIND OF AN ODD NICKNAME. WHO GAVE THAT TO YOU? THAT'S A REAL SHAME.
ANYWAY...

...YOU WANTED TO SEE ME IN ACTION UP CLOSE. ADMIT IT.
I ADMIT NOTHING. I'M DOING MY DUTY.
SO WAS HE.
AND, OFF THE RECORD, IF I HEAR OF ANOTHER INNOCENT BEING PUT IN HARM'S WAY JUST TO ADVANCE SOME POINTLESS MILITARY AGENDA...
...THERE WILL BE CONSEQUENCES.
SO, GOOD TALK, EH? I DO ENJOY THESE HEART-TO-HEARTS...
AND A LITTLE CAREER ADVICE... STICK TO YOUR AREA OF EXPERTISE.
THINK ABOUT IT, GENERAL.
PEACE OUT.

PRETTY GOOD LIKENESS...

...SOMEBODY FILL ME IN. IS "ICE SCULPTOR" AN ACTUAL PROFESSION?

AH, WELL. PROBABLY A ZEN THING ANYWAY.

HEY!
LOOKIE THERE...!
JAMES RHODES AND MISS PEPPER POTTS! AS I LIVE AND BREATHE...!
IT'S WAY PAST YOUR BEDTIME, MISTER STARK.

GOOD ONE. YOU REALLY ARE THE LIFE OF THE PARTY.
WHAT'RE YOU DRINKING?
OH NO... WE'RE NOT FALLING INTO THAT TRAP.
TRAP? C'MON...
RHODEY...
OH, I SEE.
NO WORRIES, EVERYBODY. I KNOW IT DOESN'T LOOK LIKE IT, BUT HE WORKS FOR ME.

SO...
YOU LOOK GOOD. NEW SHADE OF LIPSTICK...?
GENERAL TURNER...THE JOINT CHIEFS...NONE OF THEM ARE PLEASED WITH WHAT YOU DID.
WELL, THEY DESERVED IT, DIDN'T THEY? ONE GOOD TURN DESERVES ANOTHER.

IS THAT HOW YOU LOOK AT IT? IT'S NOT JUST SOME SORT OF GAME TO YOU...?
I MEAN... IS THIS WHAT YOU DO NOW?

YOU'RE GOOD PEOPLE, POTTS.
TRUST ME, I'M GONNA DO A LOT MORE BEFORE I'M FINISHED.

STARK'S BACK IN THE U.S....

...MISSION ACCOMPLISHED.
ROSS CALLED AN AUDIBLE, DIDN'T HE? KEPT CONVENTIONAL RESCUE FORCES BACK SO HE COULD SEE THE SUIT'S CAPABILITIES FOR HIMSELF.
AND *STARK*...

...HE DIDN'T SPILL A DROP OF BLOOD THIS TIME.
THAT'S TRUE. PERHAPS HE'S FINALLY FIGURED OUT THE ROLE HE COULD PLAY HERE...

WHAT DO YOU THINK, COLONEL FURY?
DON'T MISTAKE HIS ACTIONS FOR ANY KIND OF NEWFOUND *MATURITY*, AGENT COULSON...

...THE FACT IS, THEY'VE BEEN *PUSHING* HIM AND THIS WAS HIS WAY OF *PUSHING BACK.*

HE'S STILL GOT A WAYS TO GO.

BUT WE'LL BE WATCHING.

THE STORY CONTINUES IN

IRON MAN 2

IRON MAN: AGENTS OF S.H.I.E.L.D.
COVER BY SALVADOR LARROCA & FRANK D'ARMATA

ORBITAL SURVEILLANCE ONLINE. SYNCHRONIZING ENCRYPTED COMM SIGNALS...
THIS IS FURY ON ALPHA CHANNEL...

...I'M EN ROUTE TO A MILITARY CONFERENCE. BUT I WANT TO CHECK IN ON SOMETHING.
ACKNOWLEDGED, SIR.

I'VE GOT A HUNCH.
GET A FIX ON THE S.E.A.L. TEAM LANDING AT ADEN. IF I'M RIGHT...

"...THEY SHOULD BE ADVANCING ON THEIR TARGET RIGHT ABOUT NOW."

PATCH ME IN TO OUR PLANT.

ENCRYPTION SCRAMBLE LOCKED. YOU'RE CLEAR TO SPEAK, SIR.

AGENT GARRETT. THIS IS FURY--

--STATUS?

INTEL WAS RIGHT ON THE MONEY, SIR. A **TEN RINGS** CELL CONTROLS THIS VESSEL.

JEEZ--!
HE JUST HIT THE MAIN STRUCTURE! HE KNOWS WHERE THEY ARE--
TAKE COVER!
HELLO, BOYS.
EXPECTING ME?

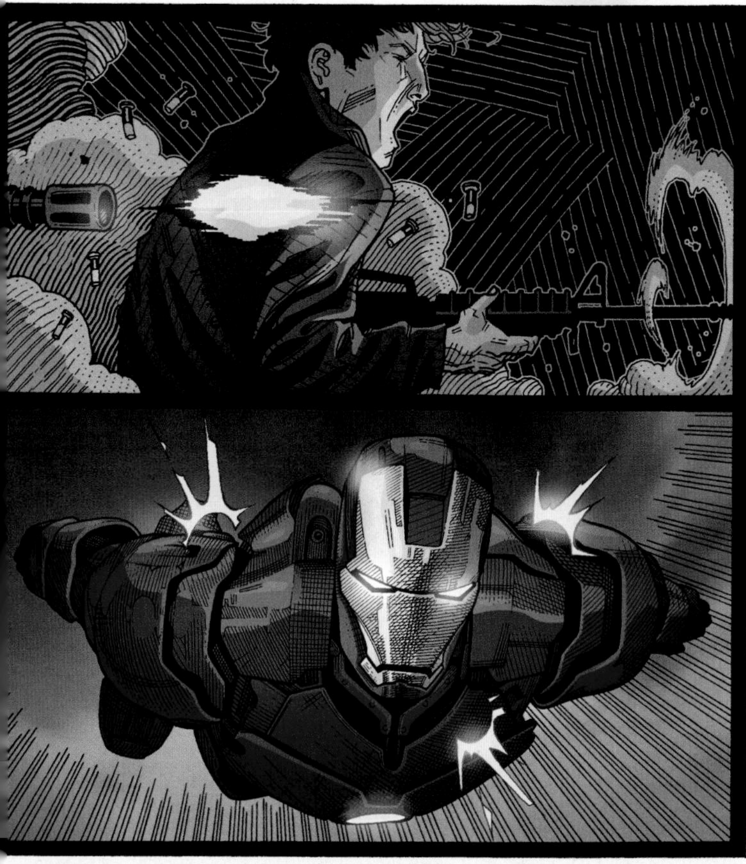

IT'S STARK--!
MOVE IN--

LET'S DO AN END-AROUND--
WATCH IT!
TEN RINGS OPERATIVES DOWN HERE, TOO!

THEY'RE **SWARMING**, GARRETT. IT'S WHAT THEY DO.
JUST KEEP YOUR HEAD AND TELL ME WHAT **STARK** IS UP TO.
NEGATIVE, SIR--
--WE'RE **PINNED DOWN** HERE!
I KNOW YOU ARE, SON. BUT I NEED TO KNOW **STARK'S** MOVEMENTS...!

SIR, I CAN'T--
MORE OF 'EM!

HOLD IT, STARK.
YOU MAY HAVE JUST SAVED THE DAY, BUT WE'RE UNDER A BLANKET ORDER TO ENGAGE IF WE ENCOUNTER YOU...
THAT'S REALLY CUTE.
YOU GUYS ARE ADORABLE.
WHAT HAPPENED?! WHY AM I HEARING STATIC ON THIS LINE?!
GARRETT--
--REPORT!
HE'S GONE, SIR. TOOK OFF LIKE A ROCKET.
I THINK I OWE HIM MY LIFE, SIR...

UNDOUBTEDLY. THAT'S WHAT HE DOES.

HANG AROUND FOR THE CLEAN-UP AND YOU'LL BE DEBRIEFED BACK IN THE STATES.

...I THINK I OWE HIM MY LIFE, SIR...

UNDOUBTEDLY. THAT'S WHAT HE DOES.

HANG AROUND FOR THE CLEAN-UP AND YOU'LL BE DEBRIEFED BACK IN THE STATES.

BACK ALREADY?

WHAT'RE YOU LISTENING TO?

JUST OFF THE FARM
MAKE SURE THEY DON'T WASH THE JET.
AND REMEMBER, ALL RECORDING DEVICES SHOULD BE SET TO--
BRRRT BRRRT
AGENT COULSON.
COULSON, THIS IS FURY...
...I GATHER YOU'RE STILL SUPERVISING THE ROGUE AIRMAN ARREST.
INTERESTING PRESS CONFERENCE AT STARK INDUSTRIES, BY THE WAY. LIVE TELEVISION CAN BE SO EXCITING SOMETIMES.

YES SIR, I KNOW. I'D SPOKEN TO HIM BEFOREHAND AND HE JUST WENT UP THERE AND...
DON'T WORRY ABOUT THAT. I'LL BE PAYING A VISIT TO MISTER STARK.
THIS IS SOMETHING DIFFERENT.
SIR...?
NEW RECRUIT JUST OFF THE FARM. HE'S READY FOR HIS FIRST FIELD OP...
...AND, PER STANDARD S.H.I.E.L.D. PROTOCOL, HE NEEDS SOMEONE TO MONITOR HIS BABY STEPS.
UNDERSTOOD, SIR. JUST GET ME THE COORDINATES AND I'LL BE THERE.
ENTHUSIASTIC AS ALWAYS. BUT I'D LIKE SOME REASSURANCE THAT YOU'RE UP FOR THIS ASSIGNMENT. IT'S BEEN A BUSY COUPLE OF WEEKS...
...YOU'RE SURE YOU DON'T NEED A LITTLE R&R...?
NO, SIR. I'M GOOD TO GO.
NEW AGENTS NEED TO BE RAZOR SHARP.
I UNDERSTAND FULLY THE VALUE OF THIS ASSIGNMENT...

"...SEND ME HIS FILE AND I'LL TAKE CARE OF THE REST."
HHHNN--!
MISTER HENDRICKS...
...I'M SPECIAL AGENT COULSON.
I'M SURE THIS ISN'T EXACTLY WHAT YOU WERE EXPECTING.
AFTER BEING RECRUITED OUT OF STANFORD... AFTER THREE YEARS OF INTENSIVE TRAINING...NO DOUBT YOU WERE HOPING FOR SOME SORT OF CEREMONY TO MARK THE OCCASION.
WE DON'T DO THAT.

YES, SIR... I GATHERED AS MUCH.
SO, I'LL BE SUPERVISING YOUR FIRST ASSIGNMENT. A BIT OF SURVEILLANCE TO GET YOUR FEET NICE AND WET.
I'VE READ YOUR FILE. I KNOW WHAT YOUR SPECIALTIES ARE. BUT DON'T ASSUME THIS JOB IS BENEATH YOU.
GATHERING RELIABLE INTEL IS AN ESSENTIAL COMPONENT TO--
BRRRT BRRRT
AGENT COULSON.
...
YES, SIR.
AND THAT'S CONFIRMED? THEY'RE RIGHT IN THE VICINITY?
WELL, I'VE GOT SOME FRESH MEAT HERE, BUT I'M SURE THAT HE...
RIGHT. WE'RE ON IT, SIR.
WHAT THE HELL--?!
FORGET THE SURVEILLANCE OP. WE'RE ON THE CLOCK TO INTERCEPT A TERRORIST CELL.
TEN RINGS OPERATIVES RIGHT HERE IN THE CITY. THEY'RE ON THE MOVE--
--AND SO ARE WE.

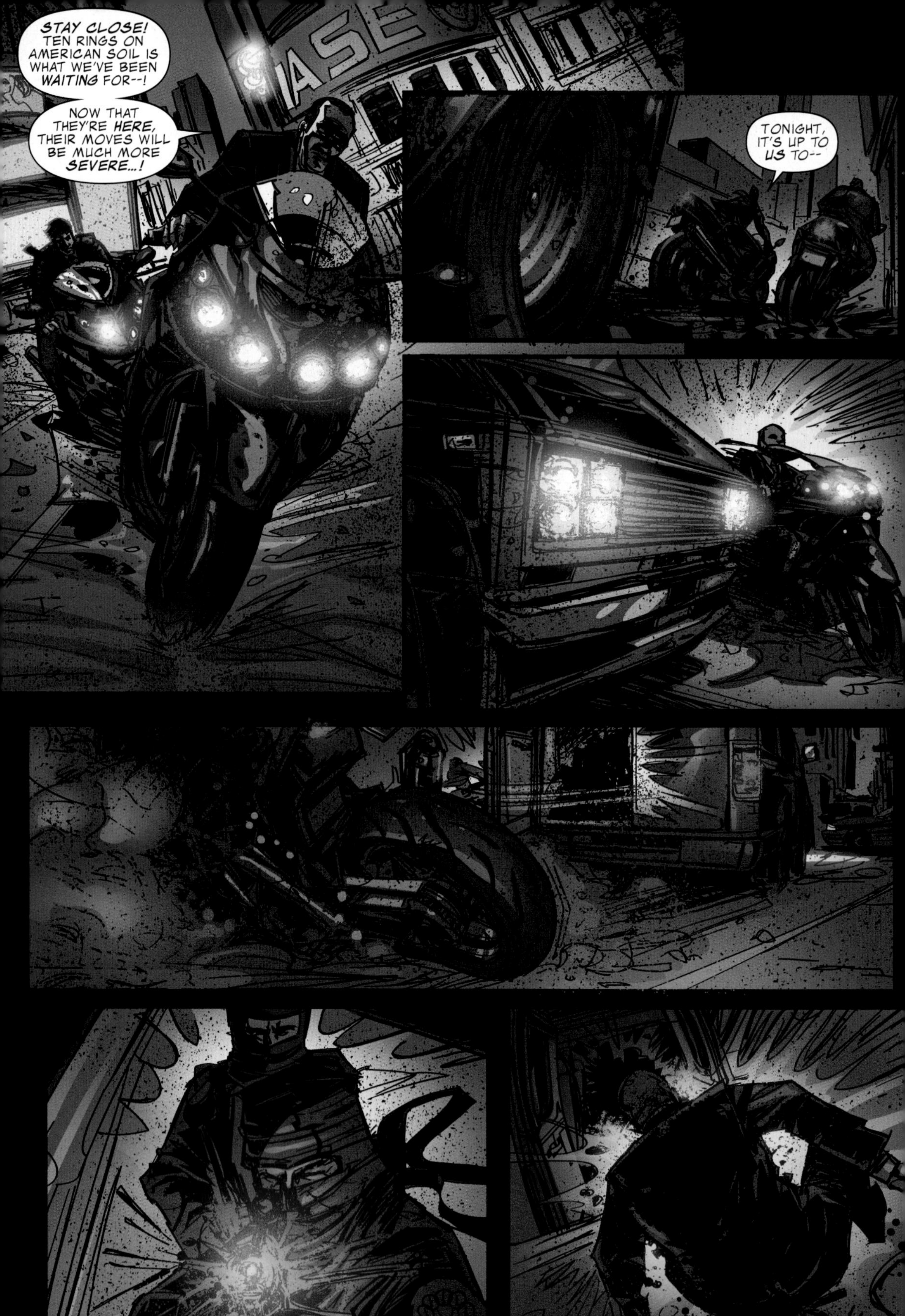
STAY CLOSE! TEN RINGS ON AMERICAN SOIL IS WHAT WE'VE BEEN WAITING FOR--!
NOW THAT THEY'RE HERE, THEIR MOVES WILL BE MUCH MORE SEVERE...!
TONIGHT, IT'S UP TO US TO--

NO--!

PANT
PANT
PANT
PANT
PANT
WHAT--?!
NO BODY--?
CONGRATULATIONS, HENDRICKS...
...OTHER THAN LETTING THE DRIVER GET AWAY, THAT WAS EFFICIENT.
ARE YOU KIDDING ME?!

I-I SAW IT...
YOU--
IMPORTANT ORDER OF FIELD WORK...
...DON'T BELIEVE EVERYTHING YOU SEE.
MORE IMPORTANTLY, DON'T LET YOUR EMOTIONS DICTATE WHAT YOU BELIEVE.
I TOLD YOU BEFORE... INITIATION INTO OUR RANKS IS A LITTLE MORE COMPLICATED THAN, SAY, GRADUATING FROM THE POLICE ACADEMY.
THIS KIND OF MANUFACTURED SCENARIO...SOMETIMES IT'S THE ONLY WAY TO KNOW FOR SURE HOW YOU'LL DO UNDER FIRE.
BUT YOU DID FINE. NICK FURY'S GOING TO LOVE YOU.
AGENT HENDRICKS.
WELCOME TO S.H.I.E.L.D.
END

...SO, WE NEED TO GET YOU EMBEDDED RIGHT AWAY. WE'LL HAVE YOUR NEW I.D. AND YOUR CREDENTIALS ALL SET UP.
WHAT'S YOUR CURRENT STATUS?
JUST A ROUTINE OP, SIR--

RIGHT. WELL, WRAP IT UP AND COME HOME.
STRUCTURALLY, STARK'S COMPANY IS BYZANTINE, TO SAY THE LEAST. THIS IS DEEP COVER SO YOU'LL HAVE TO WORK YOUR WAY IN TO GET CLOSE TO HIM.
THAT'S WHAT I DO, COLONEL--

--ALTHOUGH WHAT YOU'RE DESCRIBING DOESN'T SOUND ALL THAT EXCITING.
THAT MAY BE TRUE, AGENT ROMANOFF...

PROXIMITY
...BUT I NEED THE BEST FOR THIS.
I NEED THE BLACK WIDOW.
FINE.
JUST GIVE ME A FEW MINUTES TO FINISH UP HERE.

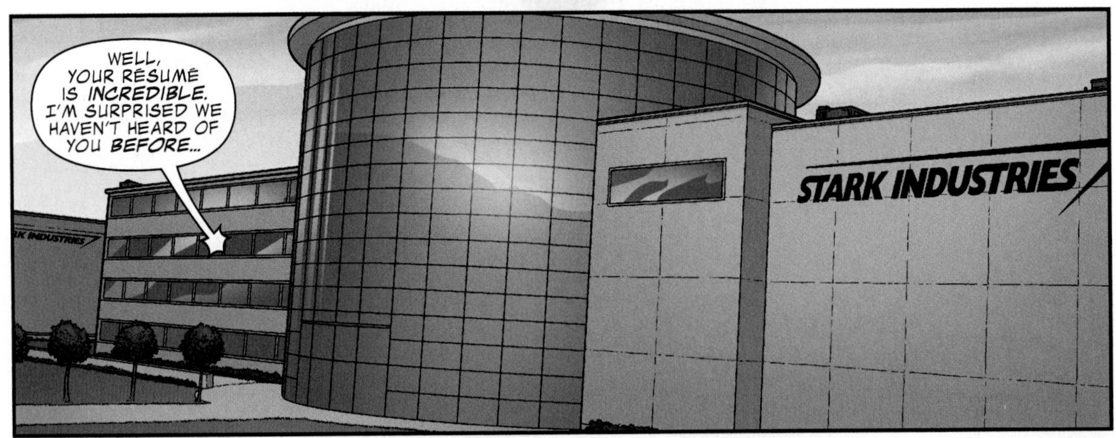
WELL, YOUR RÉSUMÉ IS INCREDIBLE. I'M SURPRISED WE HAVEN'T HEARD OF YOU BEFORE...
STARK INDUSTRIES

...UMMM... NATALIE RUSHMAN.
INTERESTING NAME.
OBVIOUSLY, STARK INDUSTRIES HAS AN EXTENSIVE LEGAL DEPARTMENT. SO YOU'LL FEEL LIKE A SMALL FISH IN A BIG POND AT FIRST. QUALIFICATIONS ASIDE, THERE IS A PECKING ORDER HERE.

KEEP THAT IN MIND AND YOU'LL DO FINE.
I UNDERSTAND.
THANK YOU FOR THE OPPORTUNITY, MRS. ARBOGAST.

CORPORATE BLOAT, ALL AROUND ME.
TWELVE EMPLOYEES FOR EVERY ONE JOB. AMERICAN INEFFICIENCY AT ITS FINEST.

SHE'S IN.
SHE'S NOT THRILLED WITH THIS ONE, COLONEL FURY.
NO, I CAN'T IMAGINE SHE WOULD BE.
SHE'LL DO FINE.

SO FAR, THIS JOB IS BEING WINDOW DRESSING FOR STARK'S LAWYERS.
...SO, IF YOU WOULDN'T MIND AUTOGRAPHING THESE. WE'VE GOT A NOTARY HERE TO MAKE IT ALL NICE AND OFFICIAL.
AND MISTER STARK THANKS YOU FOR YOUR TIME AND EFFORT.

THEY ARE FAR FROM SOLDIERS. THEY ARE MORE LIKE TRAPPED RATS.
LISTEN, HONEY...
...TRY A LOWER CUT TOP NEXT TIME. HELPS THESE MEETINGS RUN A LOT SMOOTHER.

I THINK I PREFER THE COMPANY OF TERRORISTS.
I KNOW EXACTLY HOW TO DEAL WITH THEM...

DEEP BREATH.
THEIR LIVES ARE ALREADY WORTHLESS.

I'M LEARNING FIRSTHAND THIS "PECKING ORDER" I WAS TOLD ABOUT...
...IT'S ALL ABOUT NAVIGATING THE MINEFIELD, NAT.
YOU'LL LEARN.
IT MAY TAKE A WHILE, BUT YOU'LL GET THERE.

SAMANTHA CARLISLE. SENIOR PARALEGAL. SHE'S TWO YEARS YOUNGER THAN ME.
...IT'S ALL ABOUT MAKING THAT PERSONAL CONTACT. THAT'S HOW YOU GET AHEAD IN THIS COMPANY.
I'VE WORKED HERE SEVEN YEARS AND I'VE NEVER EVEN SEEN HIM IN PERSON...!
WELL, TONY STARK MAY BE A BIG SUPER HERO BOSS--

--BUT HE'S STILL A MAN.
RIGHT, NAT?
I HATE BEING CALLED "NAT."

INTERESTING HOW SAMANTHA'S AGENDA AND MY OWN ARE SO SIMILAR...

...I DIDN'T JUST FALL OFF THE TRUCK, OKAY? I KNOW THOSE DOCUMENTS NEED HIS SIGNATURE.
SAMANTHA, I REALLY DON'T HAVE TIME FOR--

AND SOMEONE FROM MY DEPARTMENT NEEDS TO BE THERE WHEN HE SIGNS THEM.
I KNOW THESE PAPERS ARE TIME-SENSITIVE, SO DON'T FORGET WHO HAS SENIORITY IN MY DIVISION!

HOPE YOU'RE PAYING ATTENTION, NAT.
DON'T LET ANYONE GET IN YOUR WAY IF YOU REALLY WANT SOMETHING.
I DON'T. GET WHAT I'M SAYING?

OH, I DEFINITELY DO.
GAME ON.

TIME TO USE MY REAL SKILL SET...

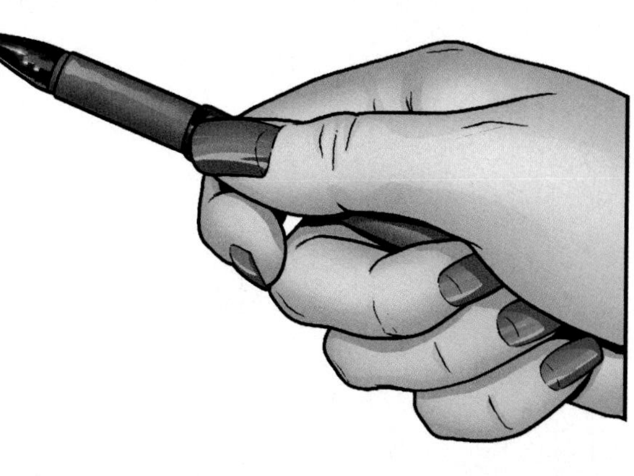

...HEARD SHE STOPPED INTO THE COORDINATOR'S OFFICE AND PRETTY MUCH MARKED HER TERRITORY.
WELL, BE THAT AS IT MAY--

--WE STILL NEED SOMEONE TO HEAD OUT TO MALIBU TODAY WITH THOSE PAPERS.

FINE. WE'LL SEND SAMANTHA OVER THERE THIS AFTERNOON.

NICK FURY WANTS ME CLOSE TO TONY STARK. THIS IS MY CHANCE.

SAMANTHA'S ON HER COFFEE BREAK IN THE DINING HALL ON LEVEL FOUR.
IT'S SIX LEVELS DOWN.

SHE'S ONLY THERE FOR ANOTHER THREE MINUTES...

...I TAKE A SHORTCUT.

MISS RUSHMAN.
WE NEED YOU TO TAKE SOME DOCUMENTS OUT TO MISTER STARK'S HOUSE RIGHT AWAY.
OH?
WHAT HAPPENED TO SAMANTHA...?

NO IDEA. BUT SHE'S IN THE INFIRMARY PUKING HER GUTS OUT.
PROBABLY SOMETHING SHE ATE. BUT WE DON'T HAVE TIME TO WAIT ON HER AND THE OTHER PARALEGALS ARE IN A MEETING, SO IF YOU WOULDN'T MIND...

HE LIVES LIKE A KING.

HE WEARS A KING'S ARMOR OF HIS OWN MAKING.

BUT ANYTHING MANMADE IS BOUND TO HAVE ITS IMPERFECTIONS.
SO... GO RIGHT INSIDE...

MR. STARK, THE NOTARY'S HERE.
FINALLY... THERE HE IS.
AND AWAY WE GO...
END

Nazi-Occupied Danish Straits. April, 1944.
GET READY!
STAND UP!
HOOK UP!
EQUIPMENT CHECK!
SOUND OFF FOR EQUIPMENT CHECK!
ONE, OKAY!
GO GO GO!!

GIVE HYDRA HELL, CAPTAIN!
CAPTAIN AMERICA: FIRST VENGEANCE
Written by Fred Van Lente
Chapter 1
Art by Luke Ross
Color Art by Richard Isanove
Chapter 2
Pencils by Neil Edwards
Inks by Crimelab Studios & Daniel Green
Colors by Sotocolor
VC's Clayton Cowles Letters
Tim Smith 3 & Taylor Esposito Production
Charlie Beckerman Asst. Editor
Ralph Macchio Editor
Axel Alonso Editor in Chief
Joe Quesada Chief Creative Officer
Dan Buckley Publisher
Alan Fine Exec. Producer
"RATATATATAT!"
"MRRREEOOOWWW-- BOOOOM!!"

ell's Kitchen,
anhattan.
une, 1924.
PKKSSSSHH!
BABOOM!
C'MON, BOYS, WE'RE GOIN' OVER THE TOP!
LAST ONE TO THE KAISER'S PALACE IS A ROTTEN EGG!
STEVE? KAFF!
PSSHHH!! POW! POW!
TAKE THAT, YOU DIRTY HUN!!

COME UP HERE A MINUTE, WILL YOU, PLEASE?
YOU WANT TO BE A SOLDIER *KAFF* LIKE YOUR FATHER, DON'T YOU?
YES, MAMA. MORE THAN ANYTHING.
WELL. I IMAGINE THAT'S WHAT JOE WOULD WANT. YOU AND HIM. ACORN AND TREE. *KAFF*
ONCE HE GOT AN IDEA LODGED IN HIS HEAD, THERE WAS NO SHAKING IT LOOSE EITHER.
WHATEVER YOU DREAM, YOU CAN BE, BUT YOU'RE GONNA HAVE TO FIGHT FOR IT.
PEOPLE ARE GONNA SPEND YOUR WHOLE LIFE TAKING ONE LOOK AT YOUR BODY AND TELLING YOU WHAT YOU CAN'T DO.
BUT THEY CAN'T SEE LIKE I DO. IT HOLDS A HEART TEN TIMES ITS SIZE.
YOU GOT NO QUIT IN YOU.
JUST PROMISE YOUR MAMA...YOU'LL USE YOUR HEAD TOO. FINE LINE BETWEEN FEARLESS AND FOOLHARDY.
TOOK YOUR FATHER FROM US WAY TOO SOON.
I PROMISE, MAMA.

"I'LL BE CAREFUL."
KKRRAKABOOOOM

"AND STAY DOWN!"

Hell's Kitchen.
September, 1930.
FOR THE LAST TIME, RUNT...
...YOU EIGHTH AVENUE PUNKS WANNA CROSS TENTH, YOU GOTTA PAY A TOLL.
TWO BITS FOR TWO WAYS.
NOT... GIVING YOU... A RED CENT... KAFF
LOOK AT THIS RUNT!
TOO DUMB TO KNOW HE'S BEAT!
S'ALRIGHT. I CAN SPEND ALL DAY PROVIN' IT TO HIM IF I HAVE TO.
NOT LIKE I GOT ANYTHING ELSE BETTER TO DO.
I'LL SAY.
HEY, WHY DON'T YOU MIND YOUR OWN BUSINESS?!
IT IS MY BUSINESS.

WATCHING YOU SHAKE DOWN LITTLE KIDS EVERY DAY IS MAKING ME NAUSEOUS.
HAH! BULLIES ALWAYS RUN TRUE TO FORM--AND I DO MEAN RUN.
I WOULDA WORN THEM DOWN EVENTUALLY.
YEAH, WHEN THEY DIED OF OLD AGE.
MAYBE YOU WANNA GO A ROUND OR TWO TOO?
WHOA THERE, COWBOY! HOLSTER THOSE GUNS! I COME IN PEACE.
NEVER EVEN OCCURRED TO ME TO STAND UP TO THOSE BUMS UNTIL I SAW A SHRIMP LIKE YOU DO IT.
YOU'RE A REAL INSPIRATION, YOU KNOW THAT?
THANKS... I GUESS.
STEVE ROGERS. BEEN IN THE ORPHANAGE ON EIGHTH SINCE MY MOM PASSED.
GOOD TO KNOW YOU, KID. JAMES BUCHANAN BARNES.
MY FRIENDS CALL ME BUCKY.

SIE ERGEBEN!
"SURRENDER?"
DON'T KNOW THE MEANING OF THE WORD.
NNNNNH!
IN ANY LANGUAGE.

<IT'S HIM.*>
<HE'S HERE.>
*TRANSLATED FROM GERMAN.
<CAN YOU BE SO SURE THEY SENT HIM?>
<OH, I AM QUITE SURE.>
<I FEEL HIS PRESENCE AS ONE WOULD A PHANTOM LIMB.>
<DO YOU, DOCTOR?>
<IT IS MADNESS TO THINK YOU CAN CONVERT HIM, MEIN HERR.>
<I KNOW HIS TYPE.>
<WE HAVE MORE IN COMMON THAN EITHER HE OR YOU SUSPECT.>
<AS I WILL **SHOW** HIM.>

Unnamed island
in Nazi-Occupied
Danish Straits.
April, 1944.

GRENADE! ACHTUNG!
WWWWOOOOOOOOOOOOO
THE CALL...
"STEVE! PSSST! STEVE!"

Times Square, Manhattan, December 7, 1941.
"SHE EVER GONNA TAKE THE ROBE OFF?"
EVENTUALLY SHE DOES, YEAH.
ABOUT WHAT TIME? I GOT TO GO TO THE CAN AND I DON'T WANT TO MISS IT.
THE WHOLE CONCEPT OF "ART APPRECIATION" ISN'T REALLY SINKING IN WITH YOU, IS IT, BUCKY?
WHAT? SHE'S ART.
AND I APPRECIATE HER!
YOU GOT A FUNNY WAY OF SHOWING IT.
PHILISTINE. YOU ARE TALKING TO THE NEXT PICASSO.
IT'S TRUE WHAT THEY SAY, THEN.
ART IS DEAD.
WAR! WE'RE AT WAR!
SNEAK ATTACK--THEY BOMBED THE HELL OUTTA PEARL HARBOR! GET YOUR UNIFORMS ON, BOYS!
WAIT--WHO BOMBED WHAT NOW?
PEARL HARBOR? THAT IN QUEENS?
TURN ON THE RADIO!

NEWS
WAR! WAR! WAR! WAR! WAR! WAR!
ALL THOSE SAILORS...ENTOMBED IN THEIR SHIPS AT THE BOTTOM OF THE SEA...
WHAT THEIR FAMILIES MUST BE GOING THROUGH...
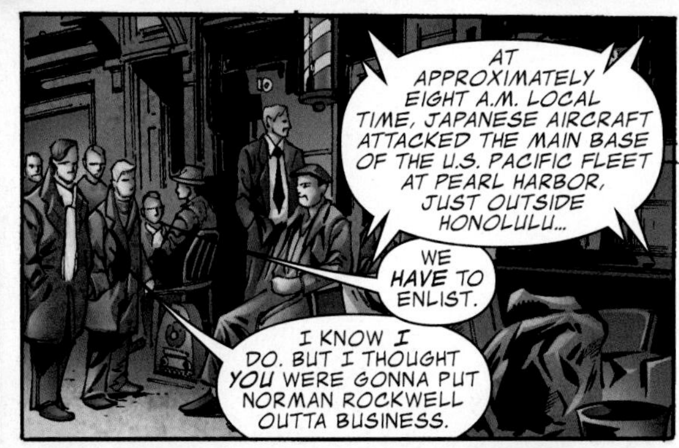
AT APPROXIMATELY EIGHT A.M. LOCAL TIME, JAPANESE AIRCRAFT ATTACKED THE MAIN BASE OF THE U.S. PACIFIC FLEET AT PEARL HARBOR, JUST OUTSIDE HONOLULU...
WE HAVE TO ENLIST.
I KNOW I DO. BUT I THOUGHT YOU WERE GONNA PUT NORMAN ROCKWELL OUTTA BUSINESS.
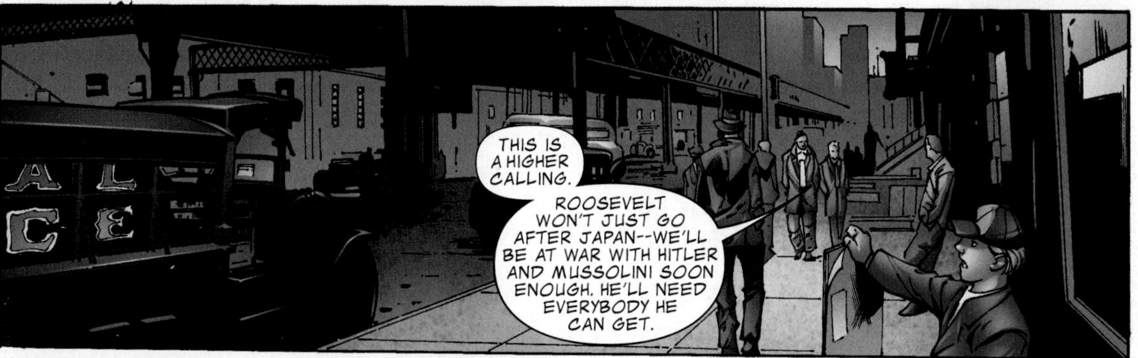
THIS IS A HIGHER CALLING.
ROOSEVELT WON'T JUST GO AFTER JAPAN--WE'LL BE AT WAR WITH HITLER AND MUSSOLINI SOON ENOUGH. HE'LL NEED EVERYBODY HE CAN GET.

BUT YOU--
SAVE YOUR BREATH. I'VE HEARD THE SAME SCRIPT SINCE WE WERE KIDS.

AM I OR AM I NOT TALKING TO THE THREE-TIME WEST SIDE YMCA WELTERWEIGHT CHAMP?
WELL... SURE, BUT--
YOU CAN GET ME READY TO PASS THAT PHYSICAL, BUCK! I KNOW YOU CAN!
I DON'T KNOW THAT! I NEED SOMETHING TO WORK WITH FIRST!

YOU GET WINDED TAKING THREE FLIGHTS OF STAIRS! YOU DON'T NEED A TRAINER, STEVE-O.
YOU NEED A COMPLETE BODY TRANSPLANT.

FORGET IT, THEN.
I'LL FIGURE IT ON MY OWN.

WHOA THERE, COWBOY.

I DIDN'T SAY NO.

December 11, 1941.
GOLDIE'S GYM
BOXING REGIMEN'S THE TOUGHEST THERE IS.

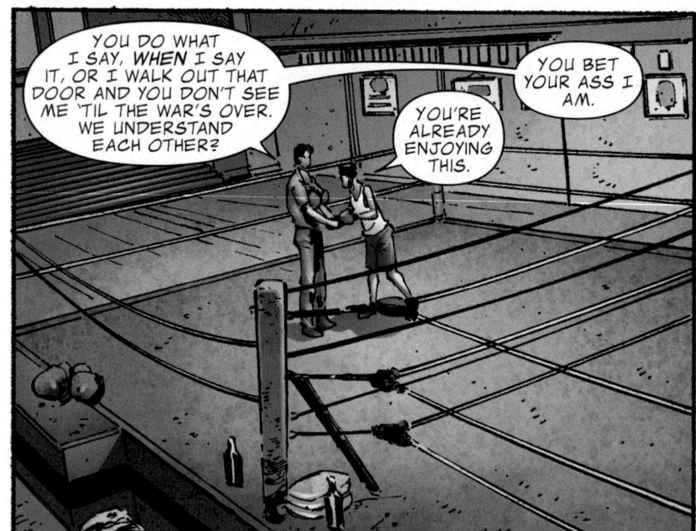
YOU DO WHAT I SAY, WHEN I SAY IT, OR I WALK OUT THAT DOOR AND YOU DON'T SEE ME 'TIL THE WAR'S OVER. WE UNDERSTAND EACH OTHER?
YOU BET YOUR ASS I AM.
YOU'RE ALREADY ENJOYING THIS.

SOME GETUP.
SO WE GONNA WARM UP WITH JUMP ROPE, OR--

AAHH!

WHAT THE HELL?!
NO WARM-UP. BASIC PRINCIPLES.
YOU'RE WEAK, STEVE. SO YOU GOTTA STAY ALERT AT ALL TIMES, OR THE STRONG'LL TAKE ADVANTAGE.

"JUST LIKE THE MANY GANG UP ON THE FEW.

"BIGGER MEANS SLOWER.
"SO YOU GOTTA BE FAST.

"NOW DON'T MAKE THE MISTAKE OF THINKING ALL BIG GUYS ARE DUMB.

"BUT STILL--
"YOU GOT TO BE SMARTER."

GOOD! THAT'S MY MAN!
KAFF KAFF
COME ON! KEEP IT GOING! DON'T PUNK OUT ON ME NOW!
December 16, 1941.

"GIMME AN UPPERCUT! GOOD!"

December 20, 1941.
HAFF
HAFF
HAFF
VISITING US FROM INDIANA, HUH? NEVER BEEN THERE. BUT FOR SOME REASON...NOW I REALLY WANT TO GO.
YOU SHOULD WORK FOR THE BOARD OF TOURISM OR SOMETHING.
YOU'RE ONE OF THOSE SILVER-TONGUED CITY TYPES MY MOTHER WARNED ME ABOUT, AREN'T YOU?

"MEANS I'M GETTING THROUGH."

U.S. Recruiting & Induction Station. Governors Island, New York Harbor. December 24, 1941.

NEXT!

KNOCK 'EM DEAD.

YOU TOO.

COUGH?
KAFF
HRM.

"HRM"?
WHAT "HRM"?
I'M AFRAID A CHAIN IS ONLY AS STRONG AS ITS WEAKEST LINK, SON. OUR JOB IS TO FORGE AS STRONG A CHAIN AS--

NO! I NEED TO DO THIS!
HEY, DON'T TAKE IT SO HARD, MY BOY!
THERE'LL BE FIVE GIRLS FOR EVERY FELLA IN NEW YORK SOON ENOUGH--
I WANT TO SERVE MY COUNTRY.

DEFEND OUR COUNTRY
SAYS HERE YOU HAVE ART TRAINING. SOMEBODY HAS TO DRAW THOSE POSTERS.
THERE ARE WAYS TO SERVE YOUR COUNTRY OTHER THAN FIGHTING.

BUT THIS IS THE ONLY WAY THAT MATTERS TO ME.

I'M SORRY, SON.

THIS IS BIGGER THAN YOU.
4F

I'M GOIN' IN THE NAVY, HOW ABOUT YOU?
NAW, REGULAR ARMY ALL THE WAY. THEY ALREADY TOOK ME!

STATIONED ON LAND, PAL, THAT'S WHERE THE WOMEN ARE--

STEVE...
I'M... I'M SORR--

DON'T SWEAT IT, BUCK.

I'M GONNA GET A SECOND OPINION.

SSSSS
ENOUGH ALREADY.
THEY SAID THIS WAS BIGGER THAN ME.
DON'T THINK THEY MEANT YOU, THOUGH.

Unnamed Island in
Nazi-Occupied Danish Straits.
April, 1944.
GNER
NDE HOLLÄNDER
NNHÄUSER
PARSIFAL
NKEN
KKRRRRRKKK
NNFF

MOOD MUSIC?

THAT'S DIFFERENT.

CAPTAIN AMERICA: FIRST VENGEANCE

Written by **Fred Van Lente**

Chapter 3

Art by	Color Art by
Luke Ross	**Richard Isanove**

Chapter 4

Art by	Colors by
Javi Fernandez	**Veronica Gandini**

VC's Clayton Cowles	**Tim Smith 3 & Dan Remollino**	**Charlie Beckerman**	**Ralph Macchio**
Letters	Production	Asst. Editor	Editor

Axel Alonso	**Joe Quesada**	**Dan Buckley**	**Alan Fine**
Editor in Chief	Chief Creative Officer	Publisher	Exec. Producer

"BOTH SPEAK TO A FAR GREATER TRUTH."
Deutsches Opernhaus, Berlin. February, 1934.
HÖCHSTEN HEILES WUNDER! ERLÖSUNG DEM ERLÖSER!

...
CLAP
CLAP
BRAVO!
FWEEEEEE
CLAP CLAP CLAP CLAP CLAP CLAP CLAP CLA

WAGNER'S LINE OF THOUGHT IS INTIMATELY FAMILIAR TO ME.
WHAT IS CELEBRATED IS NOT THE CHRISTIAN RELIGION OF COMPASSION, BUT PURE AND NOBLE BLOOD...
...BLOOD WHOSE PURITY THE BROTHERHOOD OF INITIATES HAS COME TOGETHER TO GUARD.

A DIVISIVE PROCESS IS TAKING PLACE IN TERMS OF WORLD HISTORY.
THE MAN WHO SEES THE MEANING OF LIFE IN CONFLICT WILL GRADUALLY MOUNT THE STAIRS OF A NEW ARISTOCRACY--

BUT SURELY THE OLD WAYS AREN'T TO BE DISPENSED WITH ALTOGETHER?
WHO...?

PLEASE--FORGIVE MY MANNERS. JOHANN SHMIDT, MEIN FÜHRER. CONDUCT GRADUATE RESEARCH IN PHYSICS AT THE UNIVERSITY.
HERR WAGNER'S MUSIC HAS INFLUENCED MY WORK JUST AS IT HAS INSPIRED YOU TO SET GERMANY BACK ON A PATH TO GREATNESS.
AND WHAT HE TEACHES US ABOUT OUR HERITAGE IS MORE THAN METAPHORICAL.

BAH! A STUDENT OF EINSTEIN, AND OTHER DECADENT JEWISH--
BE STILL, GRUPPENFÜHRER KAUFMANN.
WHAT IS THE LINK BETWEEN WAGNER AND PHYSICS?

WHAT IF THE OLD NORSE TALES WAGNER ADAPTS INTO HIS OPERAS ARE MORE **HISTORY** THAN MYTH, MEIN FÜHRER?
AND WHAT THE SUPERSTITIOUS MASSES REFER TO AS *"MAGIC"* IS SIMPLY THE OLDEST **SCIENCE** EVER **KNOWN**.
WITH FURTHER **FUNDING**, I HOPE TO **CONFIRM** MY THEORIES--
INTRIGUING.
KAUFMANN, ARRANGE A LUNCH BETWEEN MYSELF AND THE PROFESSOR WHERE THERE IS AN OPENING IN MY SCHEDULE.
JA, MEIN FÜHRER.
IN THE MEANTIME...
...I WILL MAKE SURE HE EXITS THE BUILDING **SAFELY**.
DO YOU KNOW WHO I *AM*, PEASANT?
I BELIEVE YOU ARE ERNST KAUFMANN, HEAD OF THE **STURMABTEILUNG'S** SPECIAL WEAPONS DIVISION--
GRAF VON KAUFMANN TO YOU.

THEY SAY WITH ITS ADVANCED ARSENAL, YOUR STORMTROOPERS WILL SOON SUPPLANT THE GERMAN ARMY ITSELF.
IT WOULD BE THE IDEAL PLACE FOR ME TO CONTINUE MY RESEAR--
SHUT UP.

I WILL NOT LET YOU DISTRACT OUR FÜHRER WITH MYSTIC DRIVEL.

YOU COME NEAR ADOLF HITLER AGAIN...

...AND I MAKE YOU DISAPPEAR.

I COULD NOT HELP OVERHEARING WHAT YOU SAID TO THE FÜHRER.

HERR HIMMLER... HEAD OF THE S.S...
WE SHOULD TALK.

Hanselbauer Hotel.
Bad Wiessee, Bavaria.
June 30, 1934.
KRUPP?
KRUPP, BRING ME A TOWEL WHEN YOU COME HERE!
GRUPPENFÜHRER KRUPP ISN'T COMING, HERR KAUFMANN.
NONE OF YOUR COMRADES ARE.
TEK TEK TEK TEK
TEK TEK TEK TEK
SHMIDT?!
WHAT DO YOU THINK YOU'RE DOING HERE? WHAT IS THE MEANING OF THIS?
THIS RETREAT IS FOR S.A. OFFICERS ONLY!

THERE IS NO S.A., NOT AFTER TONIGHT.
FOR YOU, THIS IS THE NIGHT OF THE LONG KNIVES.
THE ONLY WAY THE ARMY WOULD SUPPORT DER FÜHRER'S REGIME WAS IF YOUR STORMTROOPERS WERE ELIMINATED.
HERR HIMMLER SHARES MY INTEREST IN THE OLD WAYS.
AND THE SCHUTZSTAFFEL IS MORE THAN HAPPY TO OBLIGE.

FEAR NOT: YOUR WEAPONS PROGRAM IS IN GOOD HANDS.

...HE CANNOT BE BORN, HAUPTMANN AMERIKA.
SCHHRRAKKKKK
ONLY MADE.
RRRRRMMMMBBBBLLLLL
LET US SEE HOW WELL MADE YOU REALLY ARE...

mmersdorf, 46km south
Berlin. July 1934.
LAY DOWN YOUR ARMS! IN THE NAME OF THE REICH!
KRAK
BANNGG
BAMMM
THE S.A. IS NO MORE!
THIS FACILITY IS NOW PROPERTY OF THE S.S.!
LIAR! WE HAVE RECEIVED NO ORDERS FROM GRUPPENFÜHRER KAUFMANN ABOUT THIS!
I WOULD IMAGINE MY KILLING HIM HAS SOMETHING TO DO WITH THAT...
GRAF VON KAUFMANN HAND-PICKED ALL THESE MEN, HERR SCHMIDT-- THEY'RE LOYAL TO HIM TO THE DEATH.
IS THAT SO?
LET'S MAKE THEM PROVE IT.
KRAK
AAAAAHHHHH!!

TEK
TEK
TEK
TEK

AND YOU ARE...?
ZOLA, SIR. A-ARNIM ZOLA...

NEVER HEARD OF YOU.
I AM WORKING ON ADVANCED EXO-SKELETON TECHNOLOGY...

TO MAKE O-ONE SOLDIER FIGHT...LIKE A BATTALION...

TOYS.
YOU ARE A TOYMAKER.
I AM NOT IMPRESSED.

IT IS MAN HIMSELF I WANT TO FORGE INTO A WEAPON.
ALL YOUR BUDGET IS BEING REROUTED TO THIS TASK.

DO YOU FEEL *UP* TO THAT CHALLENGE, DR. ZOLA?

J...JA, MEIN HERR.
MOST DEFINITELY.

RIGHT ANSWER!

THAT AUTOMATICALLY MAKES YOU THE SMARTEST PERSON IN THE ROOM.
AMONG OTHER THINGS.

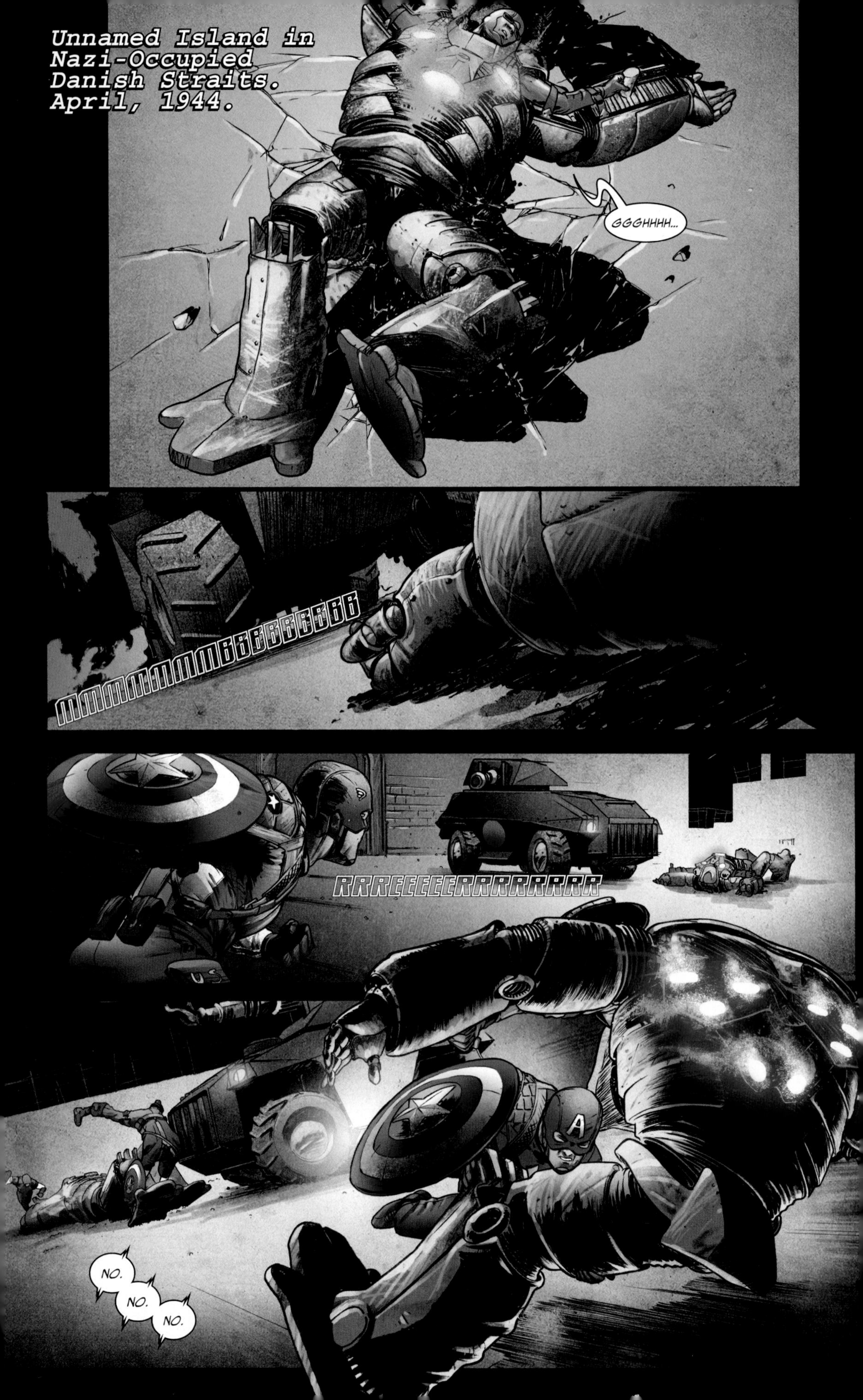

RRREEEEERRRRRRRR

NO.

NO.

NO.

ALREADY YOU FAIL THE TEST, HAUPTMANN.
MOLLYCODDLING THE WEAK IS NOT THE ALTRUISM YOU THINK IT IS.
ALL YOU'RE REALLY DOING IS PREVENTING NATURE FROM WEEDING THE INFERIOR OUT OF THE ECOSYSTEM.
AND SAPPING YOUR OWN SUPERIOR...
...BUT NOT LIMITLESS STRENGTH.

"...BELONG IN NO CHAIN OF MINE."
German/Swiss Border. September 14, 1935.
BUT I DON'T WANT TO GO TO GENEVA!
BUT IT HAS SKIING THERE, KLAUS-- YOU LIKE SKIING--
THERE'S NO SKIING IN SEPTEMBER AND THE SCHOOL PLAY STARTS TOMORROW. I WAS GOING TO BE THE MAIN TREE--
A SKI CHATEAU IS JUST AS GOOD AS A SCHOOL, KLAUS--WHY, YOU CAN LEARN ALL SORTS OF USEFUL THINGS--
ACCELERATION-- THE DRAG OF A SKIER'S MASS AS PULLED ON BY GRAVITY--
I DON'T CARE. HOW LONG ARE WE GOING TO BE THERE--
WELL-- I'M NOT SURE--
WHY ARE WE STOPPING?
N-NOT LONG, I HOPE--
NOTHING TO WORRY ABOUT, MARLENE DEAR. PERFECTLY ROUTINE. THEY JUST NEED TO CHECK OUR...
...PASSPORTS...

DO YOU KNOW THIS MAN?

ERSKINE.
I AM LOOKING FOR ABRAHAM ERSKINE.

THAT'S YOU, DA--
ABRAHAM!

DON'T!
IT'LL BE ALL RIGHT, GRETA.
STRANGERS SHOULDN'T HAVE TO SUFFER BECAUSE OF ME.

I AM ABRAHAM ERSKINE.

COME WITH ME.

YOU WAITED TOO LONG TO RUN, HERR PROFESSOR.
RUN? NO, NOT AT ALL--JUST A BRIEF HOLIDAY. I'LL BE BACK IN TIME FOR THE FALL SEMESTE--
SHUT UP.
AND SIT DOWN.
MAY I HAVE MY PASSPORT BACK?
YOU MAY NOT.

I KNOW WHY IT TOOK YOU SO LONG TO MAKE UP YOUR MIND.
YOUR RESEARCH AT THE UNIVERSITY WAS GOING SO SPECTACULARLY WELL AND YOU WERE LOATH TO LEAVE IT.
"INCREASING THE MOLECULAR DENSITY OF CELLULAR FIBERS--SKIN, MUSCLE--THROUGH SYNTHETIC PROTEINS OF YOUR OWN DEVISING.
"MY GROUP HAS BEEN MONITORING YOUR PROGRESS FOR SOME TIME, TO SEE HOW MUCH YOU COULD ACHIEVE WITHOUT OUR ASSISTANCE."

BUT THEN, SOMEONE IN THE PARTY WARNED YOU WHAT THE FÜHRER WOULD BE ANNOUNCING AT THE RALLY TOMORROW IN NUREMBERG:
LAWS AGAINST JEWS AND ARYANS INTERMARRYING...RESTRICTING THE TYPES OF JOBS JEWS CAN HOLD, ET CETERA...

YOUR WIFE'S FATHER WAS JEWISH, WAS HE NOT?
THAT MEANS YOUR CHILDREN ARE SOMEWHERE ON THIS ARYAN HERITAGE CHART, YES?

RUBBISH.
RACIST SUPERSTITION MASQUERADING AS JUNK SCIENCE.
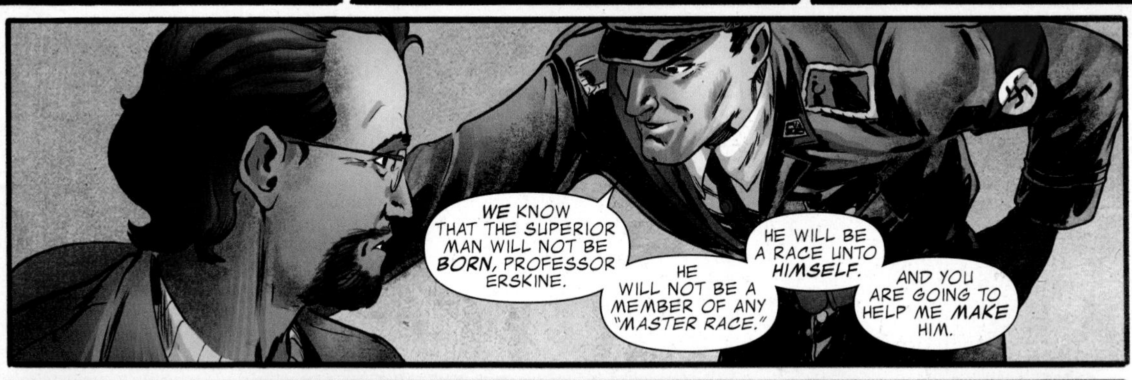
WE KNOW THAT THE SUPERIOR MAN WILL NOT BE BORN, PROFESSOR ERSKINE.
HE WILL NOT BE A MEMBER OF ANY "MASTER RACE."
HE WILL BE A RACE UNTO HIMSELF.
AND YOU ARE GOING TO HELP ME MAKE HIM.

YOU...WORK WITH NAZIS EVEN THOUGH YOU DO NOT FOLLOW THEIR IDEOLOGY?
AND?

AND IS THAT SUPPOSED TO MAKE ME THINK YOU ARE LESS DESPICABLE THAN THEM?
OR SO MUCH MORE?

FORGIVE ME, HERR PROFESSOR, FOR ANSWERING A QUESTION WITH A QUESTION:

IF I KILL YOUR FAMILY BECAUSE OF THEIR JEWISH BLOOD...
...OR IF I KILL YOUR FAMILY BECAUSE YOU REFUSE TO AID ME...
...WILL THEY NOT BE DEAD ALL THE SAME?
WHEN DO WE BEGIN?
I ALREADY HAVE.

CAP! CAP, GET UP!
UHNNH...
MOTHER, IS THAT YOU?
HA, HA.
IF YOU'RE WILLING TO GET AS SERIOUS AS YOUR PREDICAMENT...
...I THINK I KNOW HOW TO TAKE THAT THING OUT.
BUT YOU'RE GOING TO HAVE TO DO EXACTLY AS I SAY.
I CAN DO THAT.
OF ALL THE EGGHEADS I KNOW...
...YOU'RE MY FAVORITE, MR. STARK.
AW. I BET YOU SAY THAT TO ALL THE GENIUSES.
OKAY, HERE'S WHAT I NEED YOU TO DO:

AFTER
KIRBY

Los Angeles, California. February 1940.
CIRO'S IS THE PLAYGROUND FOR HOLLYWOOD'S BRIGHTEST STARS, GENTLEMEN--
Ciro's
HOWARD STARK
--WHICH TONIGHT WOULD BE YOU! WHY, NONE OF YOU GENERALS HAS LESS THAN TWO STARS, RIGHT?
TONIGHT'S PERFORMANCE IS PROVIDED BY VIBRANIUM, A METAL MY STARK INDUSTRIES RESEARCHERS DISCOVERED IN DEEPEST AFRICA!
CAPTAIN AMERICA
FIRST VENGEANC
Written b
Fred Van Lent
Chapter 5
Art by Luke Ross
Colors by Richard Isanove
Chapter 6
Pencils by Andy Smith
Inks by Tom Palmer
Colors by Veronica Gandini
VC's Clayton Cowles Letters
Tim Smith 3 Production
Charlie Beckerman Asst. Editor
Ralph Macchio Editor
Axel Alonso Editor in Chief
Joe Quesada Chief Creative Officer
Dan Buckley Publisher
Alan Fine Exec. Producer
AS INCREDIBLE AS T SOUNDS, VIBRANIUM ABSORBS KINETIC ENERGY NATURALLY!
WHAT DOES THAT MEAN IN ENGLISH? DONNA, WOULD YOU BE SO KIND?
BOOOOM

AH--APOLOGIES, GENTLEMEN, I APPEAR TO HAVE GRABBED THE **STEEL PROTOTYPE** BY ACCIDENT...
THOUGH IT WOULDN'T BE THE FIRST TIME A PRETTY GIRL'S KNOCKED ME OFF MY FEET!
CLAP CLAP CLAP CLAP CLAP

MISTER STARK? IF I COULD HAVE A WORD--
COLONEL PHILIPS! WHAT ARE YOU DOING SKULKING IN THE SHADOWS?
THE SHOW'S JUST GETTING STARTED!

COLONEL, IF YOU WANT ME TO INVEST IN A MOVIE YOU SHOULD JUST **ASK** ME. I DON'T NEED TO SEE **DAILIES**.
THOUGH-- GOOD **MOVE**, GETTING INTO **PRODUCING**. IT'S DONE WONDERS FOR **MY** LOVE LIFE.

HOWARD, THE FOOTAGE YOU'RE ABOUT TO SEE WAS JUST SMUGGLED OUT OF NAZI GERMANY BY **"AGENT 13,"** AN UNDERCOVER OPERATIVE THE BRITS HAVE PLANTED DEEP WITHIN **HYDRA**, HITLER'S ADVANCED WEAPONS PROGRAM.
OOH. THE COMPETITION.

Unnamed Island in Nazi-Occupied Danish Straits. 1944.
THE LAST TIME I SAW THIS THING, IT HAD A GIANT FLAMETHROWER MOUNTED ON IT.
HYDRA MUST HAVE DISCOVERED SOME NEW POWER SOURCE SINCE THEN...
THAT'S-- NNNFFF-- FASCINATING, MR. STARK--
--BUT CAN WE CUT STRAIGHT TO THE "MAKE BIG TANK GO BOOM" PART?
SORRY, CAP. THE ENGINEER IN ME CAN'T HELP HIMSELF SOMETIMES...
FIRST, I NEED YOU TO GET INSIDE THERE.
OH, IS THAT ALL?
MAYBE I'LL JUST KNOCK.
THEY'LL THINK I'VE COME FOR A CUP OF SUGAR.

KKREEEAKKK

SO, WHO WANTS TO BUY WAR BONDS?

WELL, THAT'S ANTI-CLIMACTIC.
THE TANK IS OPERATED BY REMOTE CONTROL.
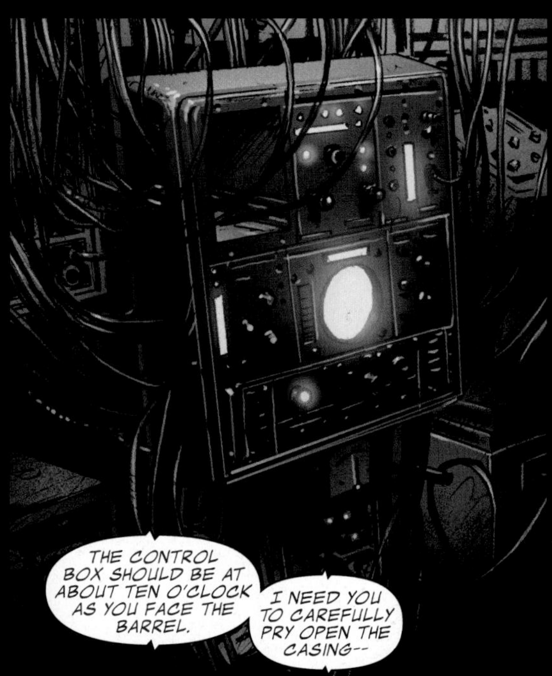
THE CONTROL BOX SHOULD BE AT ABOUT TEN O'CLOCK AS YOU FACE THE BARREL.
I NEED YOU TO CAREFULLY PRY OPEN THE CASING--

CCRAAANNNNCC
CLOSE ENOUGH.

HRRM.

HERR SCHMIDT...BE WARNED...
I HAVE LOST CONTROL OF THE TANK--

WHAT DO I KEEP TELLING YOU, ZOLA?
A WEAPON CAN ALWAYS BE TAKEN FROM YOU. WIELDED BY YOUR ENEMY.
THAT IS WHY YOU MUST BECOME YOUR GREATEST WEAPON.

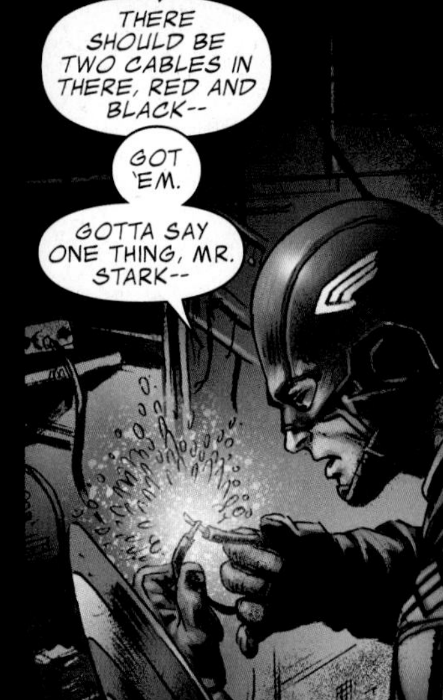
THERE SHOULD BE TWO CABLES IN THERE, RED AND BLACK--
GOT 'EM.
GOTTA SAY ONE THING, MR. STARK--

"--I'M JUST GLAD YOU'RE ON OUR SIDE."
Los Angeles. 1940.
BUT...WE'RE NOT AT WAR WITH GERMANY.
THE GENERAL CONSENSUS IN THE WHITE HOUSE AND THE WAR DEPARTMENT IS THAT THAT IS A TEMPORARY CONDITION.
THE THIRD REICH REPRESENTS THE GREATEST THREAT TO LIBERTY AND JUSTICE THE WORLD HAS EVER SEEN.
AND IF THEIR "HYDRA" DEVELOPED THOSE WEAPONS TO FIGHT SPANISH REBELS BACK IN THE THIRTIES...
...GOD ONLY KNOWS WHAT HORRORS THEY'VE COOKED UP NOW. EXACTLY.
THAT'S WHY PRESIDENT ROOSEVELT HAS AUTHORIZED THE SECRET FORMATION OF A STRATEGIC SCIENTIFIC RESERVE MADE UP OF AMERICA'S GREATEST MINDS.
HOWARD...HE ASKED FOR YOU PERSONALLY.
DELANO? HE SHOULD KNOW BETTER.
IF I'M NOT IN A MACHINIST'S SHOP OR CHATTING UP A CIGARETTE GIRL, I'M AFRAID I DON'T KNOW WHAT TO DO WITH MYSELF.
SOUNDS LIKE YOU'RE STARTING A CRUSADE. WHAT YOU NEED ARE CRUSADERS.
WOO WOO WOO WOO WOO
AND THE COSTUME DOESN'T QUITE FIT ME--
PULL OVER!
TCH.
SEE WHAT I MEAN? I CAN'T STAY OUT OF TROUBLE FOR AN HOUR AT A TIME--

--THOUGH I *AM* ONLY GOING THIRTY MILES OVER THE SPEED LIMIT--

WOO WOO WOO WOO WOO

DON'T STOP!

PHILIPS, WHAT THE--

WHAT DO YOU NEED A BULLETPROOF CAR FOR? LABOR AGITATORS?
CIGARETTE GIRLS' BOYFRIENDS.
BAM BAM BAM
BUDDA BUDDA BUDDA BUDDA
COLONEL-- THERE'S A PANEL ON THE HAND REST BETWEEN US!
FLIP THE BUTTON ON THE LEFT! QUICKLY!
BWEEP

WHHHHRRRRRR
THIS IS A WET BAR.
SORRY! RIGHT BUTTON! RIGHT BUTTON!
BWEEEP
WHUMP WHUMP WHUMP

BWHOOOOOOOOOM
YOU'VE NEVER OFFERED THE ARMY ANY OF THAT--THEY COULD COME IN HANDY.
I ALWAYS SAVE THE BEST TOYS FOR MYSELF, COLONEL.
SKKKKREEEEEEE
WITH REGARDS TO THIS "SSR" BUSINESS...
...I WANT IN.
REALLY? WHAT CHANGED YOUR MIND?
THAT WAS THE MOST FUN I'VE HAD IN MONTHS...

Unnamed Island in
the Danish Straits.
April, 1944.
WHOOOOOOOOOOOM
KRRAAKKZZZZZZZZZ
WAAHHHOOOOO!
YOU'RE ENJOYING THIS FAR TOO MUCH, SON.

WITH RESPECT, MR. STARK--
--I THINK I'M ENJOYING IT JUST THE RIGHT AMOUNT.
HRRRM.
ALL GOOD THINGS COME TO AN END.
SKEEEEEEEEE--
COMPLICATION?
'FRAID SO.
UNLESS HYDRA INVENTED A TANK THAT CAN FLOAT.
IF THEY HAVE, TRY AND SWIPE THE PLANS FOR ME, WOULD YOU?
<HOLD YOUR POSITIONS.>
<DON'T FIRE UNTIL YOU SEE THE WHITES OF HIS HELMET WINGS.>
<I WANT TO MAKE SURE...>

Castle Kaufmann.
Bavarian Alps.
November, 1940.
"...HE SUFFERS ALL APPROPRIATE AGONY."
EEEEYYAAAGGGHHHH!!

H-HERR SCHMIDT...?

I-IT'S BEEN ALMOST TWO DAYS SINCE THE, AH...ACCIDENT...
Y-YOU REALLY NEED TO EAT SOMETHING...
NYYEEGG... GGGGGGGG...

"ACCIDENT?" "ACCIDENT?"

THERE ARE NO ACCIDENTS!

WHAMMMMM
GO TO HELL!!
AND LEAVE ME...
TO CONTEMPLATE...
THE MEANING OF MY FATE...
YOU PICKED A MOST INOPPORTUNE TIME TO BECOME A FAILURE, HERR ERSKINE.
BUT I KNEW YOU WOULD FAIL.
ALL I WOULD HAVE TO DO IS BIDE MY TIME.
AND AN OPPORTUNITY FOR ME TO PROVIDE A TECHNOLOGICAL SOLUTION TO THE ÜBERMENSCH SOLDIER PROGRAM WOULD PRESENT ITSELF.
TCH.
TCH.
TCH.

YOU...ARE MISTAKEN, DR. ZOLA.
MY SERUM DID NOT FAIL.
IT DID... EXACTLY WHAT I DESIGNED IT TO DO...

"...IT ENHANCES... WHAT IS ALREADY WITHIN.
"IT IS HERR SCHMIDT...WHO HAS FAILED...
"...AT BEING HUMAN."
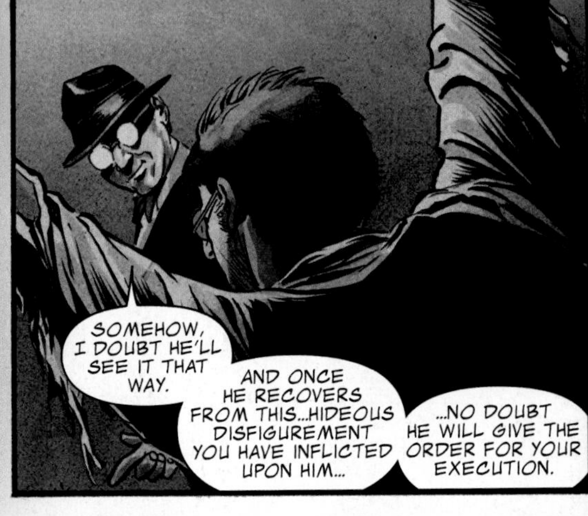
SOMEHOW, I DOUBT HE'LL SEE IT THAT WAY.
AND ONCE HE RECOVERS FROM THIS...HIDEOUS DISFIGUREMENT YOU HAVE INFLICTED UPON HIM...
...NO DOUBT HE WILL GIVE THE ORDER FOR YOUR EXECUTION.

AND HIS NEXT CALL WILL BE TO THE CAMP WHERE YOUR FAMILY IS HELD.
HOW DOES IT FEEL, ABRAHAM?
TO HAVE YOUR HUBRIS BE RESPONSIBLE FOR THE DEATHS OF YOUR WIFE AND CHILDREN?
N...NOOOO...

DOCTOR ZOLA?
DINNER IS SERVED.

COMING, EVA...
ZOLA-- ARNIM-- PLEASE, NO--

I'M AGENT THIRTEEN, DOCTOR-- BRITISH SECRET INTELLIGENCE.

CAN YOU WALK ON YOUR OWN?

JA, I THINK SO...

GOOD.

I JUST HOPE CONTROL DIDN'T WAIT TOO LONG TO GIVE ME THE ORDER TO EXTRACT YOU.

NOT THAT WAY, DOCTOR-- WE'RE GOING UP!

QUICKLY, BEFORE THE REMAINING TWENTY PERCENT OF THE CASTLE'S STAFF FINDS US!

WHAT? UP?

THAT WAS IN 1937.
SCHMIDT NEVER BOTHERED TO TELL YOU. SO HE'D STILL HAVE LEVERAGE.

COME WITH ME, THOUGH, AND--
KLK-CLAK

NO.
I AM GOING BACK DOWN THERE.
I AM GOING TO GIVE THAT MURDERING SWINE SCHMIDT WHAT HE DESERVES.
AND YOU ARE NOT GOING TO STOP ME.

DO NOT THROW YOUR LIFE AWAY, ERSKINE! SCHMIDT'S STRENGTH-- THANKS TO YOU-- IS UNBELIEVABLE. I'VE SEEN IT. YOU WON'T STAND A CHANCE AGAINST HIM, NO MATTER HOW MANY GUNS YOU BRING WITH YOU.

TAKE YOUR SERUM TO THE ALLIES, WHERE IT CAN BE TURNED AGAINST HYDRA!
THAT'S HOW YOU GET BACK AT A MAN LIKE SCHMIDT--
I REGRET I EVER DISCOVERED THE DAMN THING...

MAKE THE AXIS REGRET IT.

HOLD TIGHT.
WHY CAN'T YOU DO ANYTHING I ACTUALLY UNDERSTAND?

OOOOHHHHH!!

WELCOME ABOARD, ABE.
TO THE PLANE AND THE TEAM.
I...I DON'T...
HOWARD... STARK? I...HAVEN'T SEEN YOU...SINCE THAT ENGINEERING CONFERENCE IN GENEVA IN '34...
WHAT ARE YOU DOING HERE?
SERVING MY COUNTRY IN THE STRATEGIC SCIENCE RESERVE.
I KNOW, I'M AS SHOCKED AS YOU.

"I WAS RATHER HOPING YOU MIGHT JOIN US."
N--
WHOOOOOOOM!
AWRIGHT, HOWLING COMMANDOS--
SOMEBODY GIVE ME A "WAHOO!"

Top-Secret Hydra Weapons Facility. Austrian Alps. October 1943.
DO YOU KNOW WHY THE REICH IS DESTINED TO WIN THIS WAR, CORPORAL?
SURELY THE ADVANCED ARSENAL DEVELOPED HERE BY HYDRA WILL TURN THE TIDE IN OUR FAVOR, COLONEL LOHMER?
OH, THAT HELPS--MAKE NO DOUBT. THAT HELPS.
BUT THAT MERELY SPEEDS THE INEVITABLE.
PRISONER #49275! THIS WAY, LIMEY!
PRISONNIER #03691! VENEZ ICI!
IN YOUR KENNEL, YOU DOGS.
THE REICH SHALL WIN BECAUSE WE ARE UNIFIED.
IN BLOOD AS IN PURPOSE.
WHILE OUR ENEMIES...

"...ARE THE POLYGLOT PEASANTS OF EUROPE AND THE MONGREL MASSES OF NORTH AMERICA.
"YOU SEE, THEN, THE GENIUS OF SPLITTING UP THE PRISONERS BY NATIONALITY WHEN THEY ARRIVE."
DUGAN.
ME AN' JIMMY, HERE, 'RE WITH THE FIGHTING IRISH OF THE 69TH.
NEW YORK FREAKIN' CITY. HOPE YOU DON'T GOT A PROBLEM WITH THAT.
KAFF KAFF
JONES. MACON, GEORGIA.
92ND INFANTRY. ALL BLACK. ALL PROUD.
FALSWORTH. OF THE BIRMINGHAM FALSWORTHS.
THAT'S IN ENGLAND.
YEAH, THANKS. YOUR NOSE SCRAPIN' THE CEILING KINDA GAVE IT AWAY.
I AM... WHAT IS LEFT OF HIS MAJESTY'S 3RD INDEPENDENT PARACHUTE BRIGADE.
DERNIER. MY PEOPLE WERE RESISTING THE NAZI OCCUPIERS IN MARSEILLES.
HEY, JONES.
YOU KNOW HOW MANY FRENCHMEN IT TAKES TO DEFEND PARIS?
WHAT'S THAT, DUGAN?
HOW MANY, DUGAN?
I DUNNO.
THEY'VE NEVER TRIED.

"THEY CANNOT TURN AGAINST US WHILE THEY ARE AT EACH OTHER'S THROATS.
"AND HATRED DOES SO FOCUS THEM AT THEIR WORK."
KOF KOF KOF KOF
AMÉRICAIN-- LOOK OU--
KRRRAAANNNG

DUMMKOPF!
SORRY ABOUT THAT, FRITZIE-- KOFF--CAN'T QUITE SHAKE THIS DAMN-- KOFF
THINK... I CAUGHT-- KOFF--PNEUMONIA ON THE BATTLEFIELD--
YOU WOULDN'T HAPPEN TO HAVE A--KOFF--DOCTOR IN THIS DUMP-- KOFF
WE DO.
KANNGG
I AM HIM.
JIMMY! YOU DIRTY--
AND THIS IS THE CURE FOR WHAT AILS YOU.
KANNGG
KANNGG
KANNGG

WELL--I'D SAY IT'S WALKING PNEUMONIA...
...EXCEPT CONTUSIONS AND BROKEN RIBS HAVE TAKEN CARE OF THE "WALKING" PART.
IF FRITZIE MAKES HIM WORK TOMORROW, I GUARANTEE HE WON'T LAST HIS SHIFT.

THAT BASTARD LOHMAN WON'T THINK TWICE ABOUT IT! HE GIVES SLAVE DRIVERS A BAD NAME!
KLEIBER HAS MORNING SHIFT--AND HE AT LEAST IS PARTLY HUMAN--

BUT THEN LOHMAN COMES ON THE FLOOR AT NOON! HE'LL DRAG JIMMY OUTTA HERE, AND THEN HE'S KAPUT!
HOLD ON...

...DERNIER, YOU WERE AN EXPLOSIVES EXPERT WITH THE PARTISANS, RIGHT?
OUI.
AND YOU'RE ON SHELL DUTY AGAIN TOMORROW, RIGHT, DUGAN? CAN YOU KNICK SOME OF THAT GUNPOWDER?
FIVE-FINGER DISCOUNT'S WHAT LANDED ME IN JUVENILE HALL, LIMEY.

GOOD. AND YOU HAVE THE POWER CELLS, YES, JONES?
SO?
MY SPECIALTY IN THE BRIGADE WAS STRATEGY. I THINK WE CAN TAKE CARE OF LOHMER ONCE AND FOR ALL...
...BUT IT WILL REQUIRE US WORKING IN TANDEM.

WHY, LORD FALSWORTH--
--WHAT TOOK YOU SO LONG TO ASK?

COUGH
HERE YOU ARE.
FOR GOD'S SAKE, DON'T BLOW YOURSELF UP.
NATURELLEMENT.
KLEIBER-- I DON'T SEE THAT CLUMSY OAF #56898--
HE IS VERY SICK, HERR LOHMER, INCAPABLE OF WORKI--
I'LL BE THE JUDGE OF THAT, LIEUTENANT!

THAT LAZY GOOD-FOR-NOTHING WILL DIE AT HIS *POST* IF HE HAS TO!
I'LL DRAG HIM OUT OF HIS CELL *MYSELF*...
LET'S *GO*, BRITISHER! WE NEED THAT SCRAP ACROSS THE FLOOR **NOW**! SCHNELL!
RIGHT-O, LT. KLEIBER, SIR...
RRRRMMMMMMMMMM

FFFFFSSSSSSSSSSS
FFZKKRKLLKK
WUBOOOOOOOM
WH--
AAAAOOOOOOOOO!!!

HEY--HEY, JIMMY.
THAT CREEP LOHMER AIN'T GONNA BOTHER YOU--OR ANYONE ELSE NO MORE.
THEY CAN'T TELL IT WASN'T ANYTHING OTHER THAN OLD EQUIPMENT, SO WE JUST GOTTA GO WITHOUT RATIONS FOR A WEEK.

IT WAS WORTH IT JUST TO HEAR THAT BASTARD HOWL, JIMMY-BOY.

BLAST IT, DUGAN, YOU DUM-DUM--HOW MANY TIMES I GOT TO TELL YOU--
NO ONE, AND I MEAN NO ONE, CALLS ME "JIMMY."
YOUR MAMA NAMED YOU JAMES, DIDN'T SHE?

JAMES BUCHANAN BARNES.
THAT'S WHY THEY CALL ME BUCKY.

WAHOOOOOOO!!
Unnamed Island in Nazi-Occupied Danish Straits. April 1944.
YOUR COMMANDOES ALWAYS FIGHT THIS WELL AS A SINGLE UNIT, DUGAN?
LIKE WE WERE SEPARATED AT BIRTH, CAP.

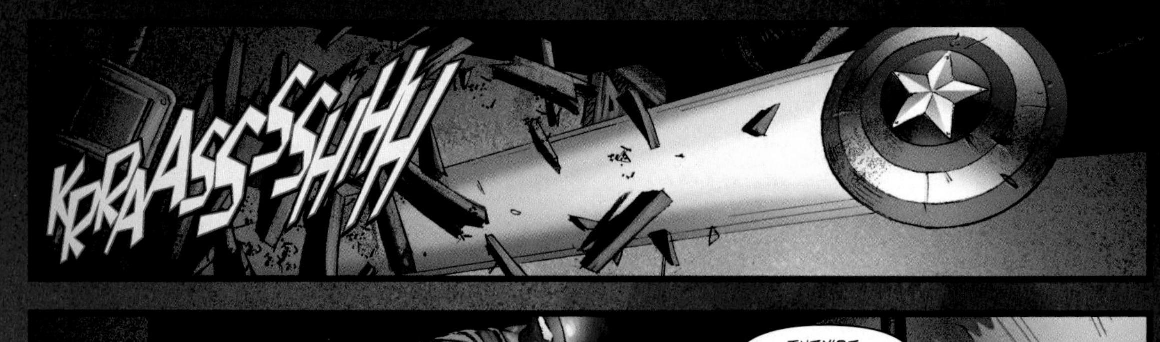

CAPTAIN AMERICA: FIRST VENGEANCE

Written by Fred Van Lente

Chapter 7		Chapter 8	
Art by **Luke Ross**	Colors by **Richard Isanove**	Art by **Rich Elson**	Colors by **Sotocolor**

VC's Clayton Cowles	**Tim Smith 3**	**Charlie Beckerman**	**Ralph Macchio**
Letters	Production	Asst. Editor	Editor

Axel Alonso	**Joe Quesada**	**Dan Buckley**	**Alan Fine**
Editor in Chief	Chief Creative Officer	Publisher	Exec. Producer

For Marvel Studios

Kevin Feige	**Stephen Broussard**	**Brad Winderbaum**	**Will Corona Pilgrim**
President	SVP Production & Development	Director of Special Projects	Creative Manager

Red Hook, Brooklyn. 1942.
PROJECT: REBIRTH.
AT LAST.

FINISHED...
I STILL PREFER "THE BROOKLYN PROJECT." COLONEL PHILIPS.
LET THAT STUCK-UP JERK OPPENHEIMER AND HIS CREW AT LOS ALAMOS KNOW THEY'VE GOT COMPETITION.
I KNOW, STARK, I HEARD YOU THE FIRST SEVENTEEN TIMES.

AND YOU ARE GETTING AHEAD OF YOURSELF, ABE. THE PROJECT ISN'T FINISHED. NOT BY A LONG SHOT.
YOU STILL NEED A MAN TO BE "REBORN" IN THIS GLORIFIED CRADLE YOU BUILT.
DO YOU HAVE AN OPINION ON THE MATTER, AGENT 13?

ONLY THAT YOU NEED TO CHOOSE YOUR "SUPER-SOLDIER" RIGHT THE FIRST TIME.
I'VE SEEN FIRSTHAND WHAT THAT POWER CAN DO IN THE WRONG HANDS.

I AGREE WITH MS. CARTER.
NONE OF THE CANDIDATES YOU'VE FORWARDED ARE SUITABLE.
WHAT? YOU'RE REJECTING ALL TWENTY OF THEM? YOUR STANDARDS MAY BE TOO HIGH, ABRAHAM.

NO...

"...THEY MUST BE THE HIGHEST."
YES, PLEASE, DO ENTER, CAPTAIN.
Unnamed Island in Nazi-Occupied Danish Straits. 1944.
LEARN IF YOU ARE WORTHY OF STANDING BY MY SIDE.
STAND BY YOUR SIDE? WHY WOULD I DO THAT, SKULL?
PEOPLE MIGHT THINK WE KNOW EACH OTHER.

YOU KNOW NOTHING.
WHA...?

KRRRRAAASSSHHHH
UNNNNHH!

MY COLLEAGUE DOCTOR ZOLA CALLS THIS A "SONOGRAM"--AN IMAGE FORMED OF SOUND WAVES.

I AM AFRAID MY DUTIES AT HYDRA ARE FAR TOO PRESSING FOR ME TO ATTEND YOUR FINAL TRIAL IN PERSON.

I HAVE REMOTELY SENT A CATASTROPHIC SURGE THROUGH THESE VITA-BATTERIES.
HAVING GLEANED ALL I CAN FROM THIS SITE, AND THE ARTIFACTS I FOUND HERE...
...I WILL DESTROY IT, I THINK. AND YOU WITH IT.
UNLESS...
...YOU LEAVE IMMEDIATELY. WITH YOUR ENHANCED SPEED YOU, AND ONLY YOU, SHOULD BE ABLE TO OUTRACE THE BLAST.
EMBRACE YOUR SUPERIORITY, HAUPTMANN. LEAVE YOUR INFERIORS TO THEIR DOOM.
OR PERISH WITH THEM.
THESE ARE YOUR ONLY CHOICES.

Camp Lehigh, New York. 1942.

THESE ARE THE FINEST SUBJECTS THIS MAN'S ARMY HAS TO OFFER, PROFESSOR.

TIME TO MAKE YOUR *CHOICES*.

...

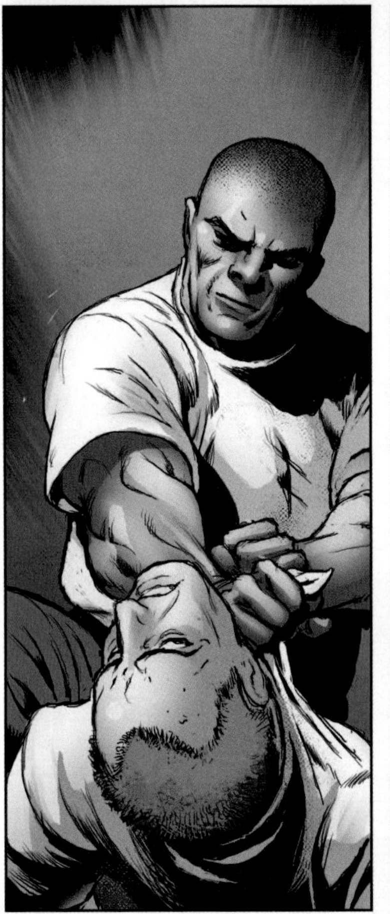

I...
I JUST DON'T KNOW...
THE SERUM BRINGS OUT WHAT IS INSIDE...AND I MUST SOMEHOW SEE INSIDE THEM--
LOOK. ABRAHAM. THIS CAN'T BE EASY. I UNDERSTAND.
BUT WE DON'T HAVE TIME FOR PERFECT. ROOSEVELT WANTS "PROJECT: REBIRTH" OPERATIONAL YESTERDAY.

AND IF YOU CAN'T DECIDE ON A CANDIDATE, I'LL DECIDE FOR YOU--

WITH ALL DUE RESPECT, COLONEL...
...YOU WILL NOT.

THE KNOWLEDGE OF THE SERUM IS UP HERE. AND ONLY HERE. I NEVER WROTE IT DOWN SO SCHMIDT HAD NO CHOICE BUT TO KEEP ME ALIVE.

SO THE CHOICE IS MINE ALONE.
AND I CANNOT REST UNTIL I MAKE IT.

DUGAN, GET YOUR GUYS OUT OF HERE!
NO, HE'S RIGHT, CAP--YOU SHOULD SAVE YOURSELF--
NEGATIVE, SOLDIER!
I'M SAVING EVERYBODY!
KRNNCH
SPAK
HELL WAS THAT BIG ROCK IN THERE, ANYWAY?
A RUNESTONE-- A MARKER VIKINGS AND OTHER SCANDINAVIAN PEOPLE DEDICATED TO THEIR GODS IN--

BUMWHHOOOOOOOOOOOM
CAP, EGGHEAD JONESY WAS TELLING US THAT SHINY ROCK COMES FROM SOME NEVER-NEVER LAND.
THAT FAIRY STORY MAKE ANY SENSE TO YOU? S.S.R. GIVE YOU ANY INTEL AS TO WHAT SKULL-FACE AND HIS HYDRA MANIACS ARE UP TO?
THAT'S OUR MISSION. TO FIND OUT, SERGEANT.
AND WHEN WE DO LEARN WHAT SCHMIDT HAS PLANNED--
--MAKE SURE HE FAILS.

World Exposition of Tomorrow, Queens, NY. 1942.
ARMED SERVICES RECRUITMENT
ARMY TODAY! YOUR DUTY TRY IT ON FOR SIZE!
HRM.
YOU DON'T THINK I CAN DO IT, BUCKY. YOU DON'T THINK I CAN PULL MY OWN WEIGHT.
WHAT WEIGHT?
THIS AIN'T A BACK ALLEY SCRAP, STEVE. IT'S A WAR.
NO, IT'S THE WAR. THE WAR WE CAN'T LOSE.
THIS IS THE ONE THAT COUNTS...
...AND I MEAN TO BE COUNTED.

DOCTOR... WHAT CAN YOU TELL ME ABOUT THAT MAN?
HE'S A FRAUD, I CAN TELL YOU THAT.
ARMY HAS A FILE ON HIM AS THICK AS YOUR ARM--"STEVE ROGERS."
TRIED TO ENLIST IN FOUR DIFFERENT CENTERS IN THE TRI-STATE AREA, CLAIMING TO BE FROM A DIFFERENT STATE EACH TIME.
THIS IS THE FIFTH, AND WE'LL PUT A STOP TO THIS, RIGHT--
NO.
LET ME TALK TO HIM FIRST.
STEVE ROGERS
BUT-- LYING TO AN ARMY RECRUITER IS A SERIOUS CRIME--
SO WOULD BE LOSING THIS WAR.
AND THIS YOUNG MAN MAY BE EXACTLY WHAT WE NEED.
SO.
YOU WANT TO BE A FIGHTER, HEH?
TO BE CONTINUED in CAPTAIN AMERICA: THE FIRST AVENGER!

BY RYAN MEINERDING